WHY THE HOMELESS DON'T HAVE HOMES AND WHAT TO DO ABOUT IT

WHY THE HOMELESS DON'T HAVE HOMES AND WHAT TO DO ABOUT IT

Micheal Elliott

The Pilgrim Press
Cleveland, Ohio

The Pilgrim Press, Cleveland, Ohio 44115
© 1993 by Micheal Elliott

Names have been changed to protect privacy
Biblical quotations are from the New Revised Standard Version of the Bible, © 1989 by the Division of Christian Education of the National Council of the Churches of Christ in the
U.S.A., and are used by permission

Printed in the United States of America

The paper used in this publication is acid free and meets the
minimum requirements of American National Standard for Information Sciences-Permanence of Paper for Printed Library
Materials, ANSI Z39.48–1984

98 97 96 95 94 93   5 4 3 2 1

Library of Congress Cataloging-in-Publication Data

Elliot, Micheal, 1956–
    Why the homeless don't have homes and what to do
 about   it / Micheal Elliott.
        p.   cm.
    Includes bibliographical references (p.   ) and index.
    ISBN 0-8298-0965-1 (acid free)
    1. Homelessness—United States. 2. Homeless persons—
Services for—United States. 3. Church work with the
homeless—United States. 4. Homelessness—Government
policy—United States. I. Title.
HV4505.E45   1993
362.5'0973—dc20   93-4208
                                                    CIP

*Dedicated
again to
Janice
Garner
Elliott*

CONTENTS

ACKNOWLEDGMENTS

This book could not have been written without the lessons I learned from many friends who were, or are, homeless. Chester Fawbush, Sonny Broughton, Bruce Barns, Lorenz Brantly, and Richard Zuzak introduced me to a world they were all too familiar with and allowed me to see it from a different perspective. Two of these wonderful people, Chester and Bruce, died several years ago, and I still miss them terribly.

Many of my co-workers over the past decade and a half shared their experiences with me, helped me to think through the people and things we were exposed to, and were instrumental in forging the nucleus for many of the ideas in this book. Janice Money, Melissa Stillwell, Donna and Rob Toney, Mark Kratz, Jim Holiday, Cindy Weber, Michael Harris, Bruce Day, and Michael Freeman taught me much about the development of a religious response to homelessness. Rodger Pack, Susan Watts, Judy Manigo, Brandie Haywood, Jacqui Anderson, Christine Harcourt, Clayton Hysell, Richard Christopher, Leslie Quarterman, Shirley Tillman, and Daniel Campbell work through these issues with me on a daily basis.

Terry Ball gave me the initial motivation to write this book. Karen Jack, Joe Daniel, and Fred Andrea read portions of the manuscript and helped me to organize it. Richard Brown and Marj Pon, both of Pilgrim Press, have done their utmost to make me look better than I am. I hope their reputations will not be tarnished because of this effort.

Dianne and Chris Fuller, Mark and Kim Berry, and Kenny and Elaine Williams provided the opportunity for good times. Guy and Anita, Bill and Kathy, Mr. Claude, Father Vernon, Cindy and Wayne have continued to be there for me for so many years. Mary Ann Beil's name is spelled correctly. I am honoring all members of the Inklings by not listing them by name.

The morning crew at the Breakfast Club, Mrs. Tommie, Georgia, Terry, and several of the cast of thousands who may or may not show up every day jumpstart my mornings. Jodi and Cheryl Sadowski, Bruce Boehme (who tried to kill me), Joel Worth, Kyle Mead, Kathleen South, and Claire (the next commissioner of baseball) Bryant serve it up right for the folks on Tybee Island. Ann Jacobs allows Jake to serve as the master of ceremonies most every morning.

David and Susan Elliott, Angi Elliott, and Margaret Elliott offer much loving encouragement. Billy Elliott is not listed with the rest of my family because he takes too many trips south without his eldest son. Providing the foundation for what I do are Jeremy, Kristen, and Chelsea, wonderful children . . . most of the time.

INTRODUCTION: WORKING WITH THE HOMELESS—CALLING OR VOCATION?

"Are you still dancing in depravity after all these years?" the caller asked. It was an old friend, someone who once worked with me actually, who had moved on and was now calling out of the blue. Discovering that I still worked with the homeless, he laughed and said he expected as much.

"Dancing in depravity?" I mused, "I guess that's a good description of what I do."

"Of course it is. What else can you do surrounded by the muck and mire of the human condition except dance?"

Dancing is a good image for the feelings I have after working with the homeless for almost fourteen years. It also describes what I do. Dances of joy celebrate every tangible success. Entertaining tap dances are for potential contributors, and slow, exhausted embraces are for those I work with on a daily basis. Critics force me to be light on my feet to answer sometimes outrageous charges. I have two-stepped around drunks and bopped with volunteers. Because politicians are always calling the tune, square dancing is often in order. I am constantly shuffling my feet to remain one step ahead of growing numbers and diminishing resources. Working with the homeless is dancing without music most of the time.

Fourteen years seems like a long time to do this. It seems I have made a career out of working with the homeless, which is something I never intended to do. I understand as much about homelessness as anything else and know more homeless people than any other group of people. My livelihood comes from their depravity, a fact with which I have never grown comfortable. This career is certainly not the one I intended to choose when I finished my education. Nevertheless I have maintained an active role in the struggle to answer the challenge of homelessness.

Throughout the 1980s America sought to respond to the most visible form of poverty seen since the Great Depression. Men slept on subway grates, women dined in dumpsters, and children slept in cars in increasing numbers. These images were captured on national television, and America responded. New shelters opened, funding for new programs was found, new organizations formed and thousands of citizens volunteered to do something about the homeless. In those years, the simplistic notion that what homeless people needed were homes became the foundation for our verbal response. Robert Hayes, former president of the National Coalition for the Homeless, reportedly stated that there were three solutions to homelessness: "Housing, housing, and housing." As the decade drew to a close, however, it became apparent that housing alone was not the answer.

In spite of an outpouring of American generosity, the 1990s dawned with an increasing homeless population and talk of "compassion fatigue." Citizens were frustrated that despite their efforts the problem continued to grow and homeless advocates continued to assail them for not doing enough. A backlash against the homeless and those who work with them has emerged. National radio talk show host Rush Limbaugh refers to homelessness as "the greatest myth in America today." A slew of new books argue that homelessness has little to do with affordable housing and that the real problem is mental illness and substance abuse.[1] For more than a decade America has tried to respond to homelessness and has yet to achieve a full understanding of the problem. It is natural then for many to blame the victim when the response has failed to achieve the desired results.

After more than a decade, too many questions have yet to be answered. What is the truth about homelessness? How many homeless people are there? Is affordable housing the answer? Why didn't the response of the 1980s work? Why does the homeless population continue to grow? How much of the problem is the fault of the homeless themselves? Are homeless advocates part of the problem? What is the difference between the homeless and the poor? What must happen in the 1990s for America to respond effectively to homelessness? Until these issues are fully examined, the homeless problem in America is likely to continue.

These are the questions I have spent the last fourteen years dancing around. In the daily effort to help the homeless help themselves, there is little time to formulate answers to deeper considerations of why things are the way they are. For the homeless, the daily questions are smaller in nature and demand immediate replies. Where will I sleep? Can I eat here? How do I enroll my children in school? From where will the money for this week's payroll come? Is there a doctor here? Can I have a job? These are the queries of the homeless in their day-to-day struggle to survive and the ones I have intimately danced with for so long.

In order to continue working with the homeless, however, it recently became apparent that I would have to stop the dance long enough to take stock of what was occurring around me. It was time to face the larger questions head-on before I could find the conviction to continue. I was uncomfortable leaving the struggle for answers to sociologists or homeless advocates alone (two groups I do not consider myself a part of), so I decided to search for answers myself.

It is important for me to note that I never intended to work with the homeless for a living. When I finished college, I planned to attend seminary, take some courses, and then settle down to the best job I could find. There was no sense of calling in this endeavor; I merely wished to continue my education in a field in which I was interested. The homeless were not part of my life, nor did I expect them ever to become a concern.

It all began innocently enough in my first year of seminary in 1979. Homelessness was just beginning to receive national attention. The Southern Baptist Theological Seminary in Louisville, Kentucky, was the site of my continuing education. My wife, son, and I were experiencing the same frustrations and difficulties as hundreds of other families who had enrolled for the fall quarter. My wife found employment at a child-care center, and I worked as a waiter in a restaurant. My daily routine consisted of classes in the morning and early afternoon, study until five o'clock, and work at the restaurant until eleven.

During that first quarter, however, I was asked to assist a small church located in the inner city with its Sunday morning worship service. After attending, participating, and feeling comfortable, my family and I decided to remain a part of the congregation for the duration of our stay in Louisville. This proved to be a good economic decision, as the congregation hired me to lead the music on Sunday mornings. The income from our part-time jobs only allowed us to accumulate debt and additional money was always needed. (In fact, my first semester of seminary was paid for with three thousand dollars my wife won at a dog track. God does work in mysterious ways!)

After a few months, however, the minister resigned and I was given the opportunity to respond to a call. The church members asked me to be their minister. I took the job more out of a sense of love for the congregation than a call from God. The story of this congregation has been told elsewhere and does not add to this effort.[2]

There were several remarkable things about this church,

however, that do pertain to my involvement with the homeless. The congregation was quite small in number, averaging around ten in weekly attendance. The majority were elderly women who had remained with their church long after it began to die. As an inner-city congregation, the church received fiscal support from the denomination, allowing it to continue a presence in the city.

Standing in contrast to the number of people was the massive building that housed the church. It was a three-story structure with ample space for activity but no programs to attract people.

Outside of the building were homeless men. Mostly alcoholics, they slept outside at night and sought shelter in the building during the day. There were not many of them in 1979, but they did constitute the powerful image later broadcast across the country. As I struggled to assume the role of minister and the congregation grappled with the fact that they had hired me, these men became a natural target for ministry.

Once it began, the ministry developed quickly. Because many of the city's soup kitchens closed on Sunday, the church began offering breakfast before Sunday school. In just a few weeks, approximately one hundred homeless people attended regularly. This breakfast spawned a daily clothing closet, referral services to city shelters, work with the mentally ill, substance-abuse counseling, and the actual provision of shelter. These services generated interest among the homeless in attending worship, and the church began to grow.

While the Wayside Christian Mission was only two blocks away, numerous homeless men found no room in that inn. Because the majority of Sunday school rooms in our church were not used at all, the congregation decided to convert one room into an apartment. After obtaining the appropriate furnishings, the first homeless man was invited to move in.

Lonnie was a small man with thinning hair and beady eyes. While he drank alcohol from time to time, Lonnie was not a chronic substance abuser. He held part-time jobs at the neighborhood grocery store and at the corner bar, which afforded him enough income to maintain an apartment for about half the year. His employers laid him off when things were slow. Whenever this occurred, Lonnie was unable to make his rent payment and would move back to the streets. It was normally at this point that he would drink. It wasn't much, just enough to make himself feel better about being homeless again. After one or two evenings spent drinking, he would clear his head and wait for one of his bosses to tell him to return to work.

Lonnie was not a lazy man. When he moved into the church building, he cheerfully volunteered to help with whatever needed doing. After a short time, he began to function as the building janitor. As the church employed a part-time janitor already, the decision was made to allow her to become the church secretary. When given the opportunity, Lonnie continued to work at the grocery store and at the bar. It was a good experience for all concerned. The church gave up an unused Sunday school room and received two employees for the price of one. It became clear that the congregation wished to expand the ministry.

Les was a sixty-year-old alcoholic who had lived on the streets for most of his adult life. He was the stereotypical street person. One morning at the Sunday morning breakfast Les announced he had not taken a drink all day. It was hard for anyone to get excited at eight in the morning. He began attending Alcoholics Anonymous, however, and in a short time he received his one-month token. The church invited Les to move into one of the Sunday school room apartments.

Like many who are homeless, Les did not have any marketable skills. Coupled with his age, there was little chance he would ever become a productive member of society again. In his younger days, he had maintained a job as a nurses' assistant for several years, and because he had paid into Social Security long enough, he knew he could receive his benefits in a few more years. Once he was sober and housed,

Les began to busy himself with the business of the building. He worked every day in the clothing closet, sorting the mountain of donated apparel, but he found his true niche working in the kitchen. Not a great cook but a satisfactory one, Les took charge of preparing all meals for the congregation. This gave the church the opportunity to again expand its ministry by offering meals to seminary students. The congregation continued to grow.

Both of these positive experiences suggested that, once given the right opportunity, homeless people would help themselves. What seemed to be missing was an adequate support system of friends or relatives who would offer assistance when it was necessary and demand accountability. The members of the congregation served as this support system. Neither Lonnie or Les experienced homelessness again.

This premise was certainly challenged in the years that followed. As other homeless men and then women were invited to live in the church, some were dismal failures, taking advantage of the church's kindness and rejecting all opportunities to better themselves. After several years, it became evident that some homeless people did not want to be helped. Because of their actions, some were actually choosing to be homeless. While not in the majority—far more succeeded when given the opportunity—these "failures" forced the congregation to conclude that the only people who can be helped are those who want to be helped. Helping was defined as a reciprocal relationship. Those who merely took advantage of the housing without seeking to contribute to the maintenance of the building were politely informed that they were not yet ready to leave their homelessness. When they believed they might be ready to work, they could again be considered for housing. Until then, however, the church would not enable their irresponsibility.

As the congregation gained an understanding of specific street people, it also developed an appreciation of the homeless issue. The lack of adequate affordable housing, under-employment, substance abuse, mental illness, spouse abuse, unemployment, and social alienation all contributed to homelessness. Yet none of these were the sole reason. Homeless people themselves were also part of the problem. Social conditions merely expedited homelessness.

Homelessness was perceived as a both/and, not an either/or, problem. The congregation concentrated on social-justice issues and became an advocate for affordable housing, higher wages, fair hiring practices, indigent health care, and additional substance-abuse interventions and mental health programs. It did not loose sight, however, of the individual's contribution to homelessness. If these interventions were going to be made available, then each homeless individual had to be held accountable for using them correctly. The congregation sought to be the bridge between the social factors that contributed to homelessness and the personal ones.

Serving as minister, social worker, and landlord to the homeless who lived in the church building, the majority of my contact with them was personal. Many of these men and women became close friends who taught me a great deal about life. The primary lesson was that "those kind of people," seen personally, are not much different from anyone else. As I wrote in another book: "They may talk differently, look different, or even smell differently, but external distinctions are all that can be made. They have the same hopes, fears, and dreams that we all have."[3] From the dumpster to downtown office complexes, there are good people and bad people in every segment of society. Given the opportunity to work to act on their hopes, and to confront their fears, the homeless will chase the American Dream with as much conviction as anyone else. They may perceive more barriers—and in many cases there are more—but given the chance and the necessary support, they can excel.

Like many groups in the mid-1980s, our group of people working with the homeless in Louisville formed a coalition. Initially, coalitions provided some safety-in-numbers comfort for service providers. Work with the homeless was perceived as new and complex. Service providers, ministers, volunteers, politicians, and others interested in the issue, each working with limited resources in comparison to the number of homeless people requesting help, began to coordinate their activities to ensure that their efforts had a maximum impact. Largely on an informal basis, most homeless advocates tried to reduce any duplication of services and to mobilize the necessary efforts to help the homeless.

At the same time, various local units of government began making funds available as a response to homelessness. Working in concert, service providers and homeless advocates were better able to access and use these funds. Numerous innovative programs were implemented as a result of these funds. Day shelters opened to provide homeless persons with a place to spend the daylight hours. Mental health programs were instituted for the homeless mentally ill. Substance-abuse outreach programs were initiated in locations frequented by the homeless. Day-labor pools were formed to assist the homeless secure employment.

The federal government formulated a response to homelessness by passing the Stewart B. McKinney Act of 1987. This legislation allocated the funds necessary to address the multi-faceted problems of the homeless with a wide range of shelter programs that cut across federal agency boundaries. It appeared that the federal government was taking the necessary action to lead the country's efforts to eradicate homelessness.

Largely volunteer driven, the Louisville coalition received funding from the city and the county government to continue organizing its efforts and to be in the best possible position to access McKinney funds. The coalition then decided to establish a staff position to lead these efforts. After eight years of serving as pastor of a congregation with a track record of meeting the needs of the homeless, I assumed the position of executive director of the Louisville Coalition for the Homeless.

My initial tasks were to organize an office, establish the credibility of the coalition concept, and convince service providers to continue working together. It was an excellent opportunity, as Louisville was far ahead of many communities in responding to the burgeoning homeless population.

The shelters worked well together and quickly developed programs to meet the needs of homeless women and children, who were now being shown on television as the newest homeless. It was purely an administrative job, however, with little direct contact with the homeless themselves.

At this point the question of my "career" became an overriding concern. The obvious thing to do for my future was to retain the position of executive director. Nevertheless, I learned that sitting around a table discussing homelessness was not the same as talking with homeless people. I missed the direct contact.

Once, sitting in my office shuffling paper from one side of my desk to the other, I was visited by Brian and Dominic, two homeless friends. Sharing cups of coffee, we discussed the new job, and I tried to impress upon them all I was doing. When they left, I didn't feel I was doing all that much. The coalition did not offer me the challenge of a community that combined people from every walk of life. It only allowed me to work with other people who worked with the homeless. One of my guiding beliefs became apparent to me: "A good test for our faith is how many different kinds of people we count as our friends. The more closed the circle, the more closed our faith."[4] This job did not allow me the opportunity to nurture my friendships with the homeless.

About this time, I took several days off and visited my hometown, Savannah, Georgia. Watching the local newscast one evening, I observed a story on Savannah's response to homelessness. It was an effort very much in its infancy. The news story focused on a shelter with a traditional "soup and salvation" approach that reduced homelessness to a moral condition. There was also a report on the city's effort to study the homeless problem and formulate a local response. I began to wonder how I might help my community address its homeless population.

The issue dogged me for weeks. Was I called to work directly with the homeless, or had I simply fallen into a vocation? I was not interested in making people feel guilty that there were homeless people sleeping outside. I was concerned about the stereotypical view many held about the homeless. It bothered me that many did not see the homeless as decent people, but as winos who deserved their lives. I wanted to help two different poles of society come together, believing that both would be better off as a result. The homeless would obviously be helped if people of means became their friends. I was just as convinced, however, that people of means would be better off knowing the homeless personally. Such relationships would enable people to share their joys and sorrows. A deeper sense of understanding would naturally occur, and a sense of balance would be struck. People of means would become more sensitive to the needs of the homeless and more appreciative of what they had. I wanted to be a catalyst for bringing together people who wouldn't normally be caught dead with each other.

I really didn't care about the issue as much as I did about the individuals who found themselves homeless. I knew that America had always had a homeless population. Throughout American history, there had always been those who chose to be homeless. I had no problems with that. America is a country that encourages people to be whatever they want. If some people want to be homeless, then they have that right. My concern was for those who did not choose to be homeless.

It also began to dawn on me exactly who the homeless were. Up until that time, I saw them as either unlucky individuals or as people who were bent on self-destruction. People began asking me very pointed questions about the homeless. How do they live? Where do they eat? What are their chances? When pressed, many confessed that they had a personal reason for wanting to know. They knew someone who was homeless. Friends and relatives of many people were known to be homeless, and these people wanted to know what was going on. It became evident to me that the homeless were people without significant social relationships. They were the truly alone and had somehow forgotten the art of remaining connected to society. Increasingly I became convinced that the single factor that keeps people homeless is the lack of significant social relationships. If we were somehow able to link every homeless person to available programs, services, or benefits, the homeless problem would not go away. It is as much the result of the breakdown of the family unit as it is the unavailability of affordable housing.

Returning to Louisville, I met with the coalition and resigned the position I had held for only six months. A sense of calling had overtaken me to start a new shelter that would not only meet the needs of the homeless but the needs of society as well. In short, I wanted to make two worlds collide. If there were a place where the "haves" and the "have-nots" could coalesce, the root causes of homelessness would be addressed. Choosing to leave my vocation in Louisville, I followed my calling to Savannah.

After only several weeks, I was introduced to members of the board of directors of Union Mission, Inc., a group that was opening a new shelter in the city. The Union Mission in Savannah was not affiliated with the national mission of the same name, although it had been at one time; the original mission had gone out of business while the board of directors had remained intact. Recognizing Savannah's growing homeless problem, the group resolved to provide adequate bed space to meet the needs of several hundred street people, and it began construction on a new facility. I was hired as the director of the effort.

To be called Grace House, this shelter would use food and shelter as an excuse to bring volunteers and the homeless into direct contact. The homeless were asked to care for the facility, doing all the cooking, cleaning, and a great deal of the paperwork. It was our goal to show that given the opportunity, the homeless would prove to be excellent employees. Volunteers were asked to use their expertise to critique and enhance the homeless workers' efforts. Both groups were encouraged to interact with the other so that the total effort was enhanced as the strengths of both groups were used together.

The results were staggering. Grace House quickly filled, and its approach was recognized by the community as reputable. Union Mission, Inc., expanded its efforts and opened the Magdalene Project, a seventy-five bed transitional facility for homeless women and children. It also embarked on the Phoenix Project, a ten-bed facility for homeless people who have AIDS. Potters Place, a thirteen-bed transitional facility for homeless substance abusers, had already been in existence but was reconfigured to better meet the needs of its population.

What made the effort unique, however, was the diversity of those who participated. The Junior League led the development of the facility for women and children. The gay community volunteered countless hours to open the Phoenix Project. The religious community drove the efforts at Grace House. The state government and local Alcoholic Anonymous groups were the principal supporters of Potters Place. At every level, worlds were colliding, each challenging the stereotypes of the other.

Observing all of this activity, it was difficult not to be personally affected by the experience.

> *I have found that the homeless experience produces a great wealth of God's grace for those who seek to struggle with it. . . . As the circle of relationships that I have made grows wider, however, I find that the grace of "creative surprise" does too. Members of the Junior League begin to challenge my stereotypes where the homeless used to. Bankers teach me a great deal about the struggle for faith. Wealthy men and women renew my sense of hope that the world can be what God intended it to be. Company executives comfort me with grace. Suddenly, I realize the community of believers is not as narrow as I thought. . . . Now I feel the world is not quite as lost as it used to be.[5]*

After several years of work with Union Mission, Inc., I am more convinced than ever that it is the lack of significant social relationships that keeps people homeless and that fosters stereotypical thinking.

There are countless frustrations with these efforts. Homeless men and women suddenly withdraw and sometimes disappear. Volunteers quit. Money runs in short supply. The number of people in need is always more than can be helped. Too many homeless advocates continue to use worn-out methods that no longer produce the desired results. Stereotypical thinking continues, and now there are an increasing number of people who blame the victims instead of the problem. It is becoming increasingly difficult to establish ongoing relationships with the various segments of society. People burn out. The number of homeless people continues to grow.

In his book *The Way Things Ought To Be,* radio talk show host Rush Limbaugh makes an intriguing argument:

> *Notice that in all of them [homeless advocates] the so-called homeless crisis is used by the left to drag down the American way of life. This is the common theme in all of them. The message is that the American people are at fault, and the downtrodden—whether they are drug abusers or homeless people—can't be at fault. You're never supposed to blame the downtrodden. Who, then, should we blame? It's true that some of the homeless have lost their homes. But the government's disastrous policies of urban renewal are responsible for destroying many of the single-room-occupancy hotels they used to live in. And many of the homeless have only themselves to blame. They either aren't willing to assume the responsibilities that go with being a citizen or they are mentally ill or abusing drugs or alcohol. Of course, we have to find some ways to help them, but is it necessary to lie to them or ourselves about their own contribution to their problems? Unless we recognize and are honest about that, we aren't going to be able to clean up our streets and help repair these wrecked lives.[6]*

Unlike many working with the homeless who write off Mr. Limbaugh, I find some of what he says, or how he says it, quite funny. But I do not agree with much of what he says. Most of the homeless people I have known personally over fourteen years have not been mentally ill, chronic substance abusers, or individuals who chose to be homeless. When critics challenge the work done to assist the homeless, however, they have a right to be answered honestly. Too many homeless advocates have made up their own facts to support their efforts or simply have chosen the statistical studies that favor their own views, without struggling for the truest possible solution.

Since 1980 America has sought to respond to the new homeless. Some efforts have been better than others. After more than a decade, however, the problem is as large and as frustrating as ever. People are starting to ask questions, many of which are legitimate. This is one insider's view of what the country's response to homelessness looks like. It is one person's attempt to take an honest look at why people are homeless, how the various responses have impacted the problem, and what the appropriate solutions may be.

ONE

DENYING THE DEMONS

"Hello. My name is William and I'm an alcoholic." The group responds, "Hi, William." Thus begin introductions at Alcoholics Anonymous meetings across the country, meetings of men and women who have come to terms with who they are. By describing themselves as people who have problems—they are substance abusers who will never fully recover—these individuals accept who they are each and every time they share their identity. If recognizing the problem is half of the solution, then they name their problem and their solution with each sharing of their identity. There are no sermons or lectures; rather, each shares his or her own story, promising he or she won't tell if you don't. Each describes where he or she went wrong and how he or she is trying to straighten out. At the beginning of each session, however, no matter how many times it may have been repeated, those who participate begin by naming their demon. "Hi, my name is William. I'm an alcoholic."

Lately I have been drawn to this image when I consider the homeless. Few of the residents who seek sanctuary at the shelters I have been affiliated with ever identify themselves as homeless. Most claim they are not like everyone else inside the shelter that night. They say they are only in-between. If they could only find work; if they only could reconcile with their families; if they could only get a bus ticket to the promised land, then everything would be all

1

right. Most of the homeless I have known, and I have known many, never claim they are homeless. To the contrary, most go to great pains pointing out how different they are from the other homeless who will sleep beside them that night.

The majority of homeless women I have met are talented. They are not chronic substance abusers, although they drink or do crack from time to time. Most are employable if they are not already employed. Most are articulate and have the ability to communicate well. Many have organizational skills, the capability to perform assigned tasks well, and the capacity to go above and beyond the call of duty. Most of the homeless men I have met are skilled and talented at navigating the maze of America's social welfare system (no small feat). The vast majority prove themselves to be survivors in the face of countless dangers on the streets. Most of the homeless children I have encountered are bright, curious, and affectionate. When presented the opportunity to better their academic performance, they jump at the chance. Most are more comfortable in a group than when left alone. In fact, few of the homeless people I have met have fit the stereotypes of winos, crack-heads, transients, the uncontrollably insane, or those satisfied with their lot. Even more amazing is that the majority have been talented individuals who impress others, improve the situations in which they find themselves, and recognize the importance of opportunities that come along.

Despite these traits, most of these people find themselves sleeping in warehouses called shelters or, if they are lucky, smaller transitional homes where they have no privacy. When presented with programs designed to help them, many participate. The result of their involvement is always amazing. Those who succeed do so immediately. Those who fail also do so immediately. The successes move out of the shelter, and if everything goes their way, they chase after the American Dream with a renewed sense of determination. Those who fail are normally propped up to fail

again and again until whoever is offering them the chance
to succeed wears out and gives up on them.

The men and women who fill the shelters of this country
do not classify themselves as homeless. The only time I
have heard shelter residents use the word is when they are
speaking in the language they know I use. When informally
asked, most deny the classification; everyone else in the
shelter may be homeless, but they are not. Why do they
deny their station in life? Why not admit they are homeless? What prevents them from recognizing they are like
those sleeping beside them? Is the denial of their homelessness preventing them from seeing the solution to their
problem? What prevents them from naming the demon of
their circumstance? Homeless people are in a constant state
of denial, and the trauma of the experience leads them to
continue rejecting who they are. If the homeless cannot
come to terms with their identity, how can they overcome
it? If the homeless do not fully understand their problems,
how can society come to terms with them?

Sitting in Norm's living room, it is difficult to believe he
had been homeless. He will tell you he never dreamed it
could have happened to him. An electrician, Norm left his
home and family in Massachusetts because of the economic
crunch and went looking for work. Not long after arriving
in Savannah, he secured employment as part of a construction crew and moved his family into a motel. Before long,
the construction job ended and he could not find another
job. Soon the money he had saved ran low, and Norm's
dream of working and having a home eroded. Eventually,
he found himself without money or a place to stay. "The
only thing left to do was regroup," he said. Leaving his
family behind in a cramped borrowed room, he moved into
the shelter.

From March 8 until April 20, Norm worked as a volunteer, then as part of the shelter staff for fifty dollars a week.
On his day off, he went to local labor pools, picking up
extra money to save. On April 21, he secured a full-time

position with an electrical contractor. After he had saved enough, he sent for his family and moved them close to his work. Today, Norm, his wife, and their four children live comfortably in a three-bedroom house. His wife works part-time in the proof department at a bank. His children, ranging in age from seventeen to seven months, are happily adjusted to suburban life. When asked about homelessness, Norm says, "No one wants that; everybody wants a place to call their own."

Several months after this episode, members of the shelter staff contacted Norm asking if his story could be featured in a newsletter article they were doing. At first, not wanting to tell them no, he told them he would think about it. When pressed, he asked if his name would be used. When asked if this was important, Norm replied that he did not want the folks at his church to know he had been homeless. He continued to vacillate until he realized he could not tell the shelter staff no. The article ran, but his name was changed and he would not allow his photograph to be used.

The denial that homelessness breeds is strong, staying with those who experience homelessness long after they have secured housing and put that time behind them. Noah Snider, author of *When There's No Place Like Home*,[1] appeared on a nationally syndicated talk show about homelessness. As one who had experienced homelessness and who had written an excellent interpretive book on the lessons he had learned, Noah was expected to be a symbol of hope for a social problem the country did not know how to manage. After listening to the heart-wrenching stories of the other guests, his turn came. Opening his mouth, he found he could not speak. Catching his breath, he apologized and said he thought he had successfully put the experience behind him but was suddenly reminded that homelessness was still very much part of who he was. Why is it that, even for those who have gotten past the actual experience, most men and women deny their homelessness? Why can they not embrace it as those who are involved in Alcoholics Anonymous do when they introduce themselves?

What is the difference between saying, "Hello, I am William; I'm an alcoholic," and "Hello, I am William; I'm homeless"?

Homelessness continues to be one of the most critical social issues America has ever experienced. It is estimated that between a quarter and three million people are homeless. In the 1990s, every major urban area has experienced a rise in the number of people on the streets. Now, we even hear discussions of the rural homeless. In addition, the people who live on the streets are changing. Gone is the stereotypical hobo. As late as the 1960s, the typical person in a shelter was male, over fifty, and alcoholic. During the 1980s, a transformation occurred. Today's street population is much younger than in years gone by, and they are without the support of a primary social network. In this country, the family typically serves as this network. Without a family or other close relationships, those estranged from their most significant connections fall into homelessness. Meaningless employment or no employment, few intimate relationships, and little hope for change breeds anger. Today's homeless are angry. Immigrants, African Americans, illegal aliens, women, children, and other minorities are finding themselves on the streets. Most still claim they are chasing a scaled-down version of the American Dream, but the security of a home is replaced by a night in the shelter. In the early 1990s, increasing numbers of young, white males began staying in the shelters.

In her introduction to *Homelessness: Critical Issues for Policy and Practice*, Anna Faith Jones includes an excellent description of today's homeless:

> The average American used to equate homelessness with drunks on skid row; now it is plain that a whole range of people sliced out of the society have no place to live. They are retired men on tiny fixed incomes who lost their foothold on self-respect when their single-room hotels closed under the pressure of gentrification. They are angry teenagers, school dropouts. They are drug addicts. They are schizophrenics lost in

an outpatient system that would baffle the most dedicated seeker of help; unemployed people who have worn out their welcome in overcrowded quarters where families are doubled up; young mothers whose names have been on the eight-year public housing waiting list for only two years. They are old people lost in the anonymous shuffle of big cities, forgotten by whoever once knew them. They are babies who have never slept in a bed or been bathed in a tub.[2]

Why are so many experiencing homelessness today? The National Alliance to End Homelessness lists the following common causes in their book *What You Can Do To Help The Homeless*:

1. *Loss of affordable housing*: Gentrification, abandonment, and demolition have reduced the stock of affordable housing. Because of changes in the tax code, very little of this housing is being replaced.

2. *Deinstitutionalization*: In the 1950s, state mental hospitals housed more than 550,000 patients. Today that number is fewer than 150,000, leaving a significant number of the mentally ill with no place to live but the streets.

3. *Changes in family structure*: There is an increasing number of single-parent households (which means that one parent carries the burden of trying to care for the children as well as working to support them). Diminished resources and support, a lost job, illness, or eviction can catapult a family into homelessness.

4. *Cutbacks in federal housing and support programs*: Aid to Families with Dependent Children, food stamps, and disability insurance income have not kept pace with the rising cost of living. Federal housing programs were cut some 70 percent in the 1980s.

5. *Growing poverty*: As many as 32 million Americans now live below the poverty line.[3]

These are the commonly accepted reasons for the rise of homelessness in modern America. Others identify the root cause as the policies of "Reaganomics." Most of those who work with the homeless would quickly agree. There are other reasons for homelessness, however, reasons that conservatives are fast to embrace and liberals immediately denounce. These other reasons are more personal in nature, yet still intertwined with the accepted causes just listed.

In my experience, people are homeless because of a rash of bad personal decisions. They do not know how to manage money. They do not exercise all of the options available to them. They prefer estrangement rather than commitment. They flee from hard work, instead of sticking to the task at hand. They drink too much. They do not recognize the available support systems. They demand more than they should and settle for less than they can. They get to the point where it's all coming together and then sabotage the opportunity. They are illiterate and don't know any better. They opt for bad friends and influences rather than good ones. To be sure, these reasons are related to the National Alliance's list. Poverty, poor mental health, or a dysfunctional family structure set the stage for most bad decisions. Still, when meeting today's homeless, it is easy to see how often they shoot themselves in the foot. While there are numerous exceptions, most every homeless person in America can point to several of these problems as causes for his or her uprooted situation.

Countless people who work with the homeless burn out for this very reason. The success stories are numerous, but they are dwarfed by the number of failures. It is difficult to blame growing poverty or the change in family structure on Jim, in whom you have invested countless hours of your time. When he fails, you blame Jim. Certainly there is enough evidence to blame him. After all, he made the decisions, or at least he chose not to follow up on the ones you made for him. Besides, homelessness is experienced in a one-on-one setting, and policy issues do not translate well to one single life. Homelessness in America is the result of both personal choice and a complex set of social factors.

Obviously, those who are more liberal embrace the structured causes of homelessness. The more conservative quote (out of context) the personal causes. Truth lies somewhere in between the systemic and personal factors. To prevent homelessness in the next generation, the systemic causes—loss of affordable housing, deinstitutionalization, changes in the family structure, cuts in funding, and poverty—must be addressed. To focus on the current homeless generation, the personal causes must be addressed by the synagogues and churches, the volunteers and advocates, and the public and private sectors. The difficulty with current responses to the homeless problem is that they do not recognize the truth in the middle.

Throughout the 1980s and into the 1990s, government has led the fight against homelessness. The vast majority of programs assisting the homeless in America are government funded. As the problem escalates, so does the amount of money the federal government spends on homeless programs. The Stewart B. McKinney Act, which is the government's mechanism of funding these programs, has spent about $2.3 billion between 1987 and 1990 combating homelessness. Roughly 69 percent of this amount is targeted for food and shelter assistance (this includes funds for the emergency shelter programs of the Department of Housing and Urban Development (HUD) and the Federal Emergency Management Assistance Act's (FEMA) as well as for HUD's other housing programs for the homeless). The remaining amount is divided between health (26 percent), education (3 percent), and job training (2 percent). These programs are designed to meet the basic needs of the homeless and to offer some options for self-enhancement. While these efforts have literally saved thousands of people from starving to death, they have made little impact on the root causes of the problem.

There are no estimates of how much money the private sector contributes to combating homelessness in America.

Certainly, millions of dollars are generated from private contributions to support shelters, church ministries, soup kitchens and clothing closets. While recent reports claim public sympathy for the homeless is waning, hundreds of private organizations collect budget dollars from their local community and from private foundations. It is important to note, however, that few programs are able to operate entirely on private contributions. Most receive at least a portion of their support from the public sector, specifically those financed by the McKinney Act. The private sector alone does not provide the support necessary for most operations.

Certainly, many will argue that a response to the homeless should be financed by the government or by the private sector, but not by both. The fact is, both are necessary to maintain the current effort. A cut in either funding source would greatly diminish the response America has mobilized thus far. It is not necessarily true that if one source is cut, the other will make up the difference. Many look to America's churches and synagogues to support charity. Ronald Reagan specifically called for this type of support when he cut many welfare programs. The end result was that the religious community did increase its level of support, but not enough to make any significant difference. Certainly its increased commitment did not prevent the drastic cutbacks in support programs. Objectively speaking, churches are having a difficult enough time maintaining their current budgets. The result has been a diminishing support from the religious community as it circles the wagons.

What is frustrating about this either / or approach is that homelessness demands a both / and answer. The separation of church and state in this country has been used to prevent a unified response to a very complex problem. From the perspective of one who has one foot squarely planted in both worlds, it comes as no surprise that America's solution is fragmented rather than unified. The response to homelessness is not simply a church / state issue; it is a matter that reflects the state of society and religion. While both have mandates to care for the homeless, the Constitution charges the government with caring for the people, and the Scriptures (indeed, virtually all religious writings) call for compassion for the poor. Each institution is frightened that it will be corrupted if it works in concert with the other. A social problem as complex as homelessness can only be addressed comprehensively, however; the strengths of both institutions must come together. The government can, and should, lead the attack on the structural causes of homelessness. It is the only institution capable of adequately addressing them. The religious community must lead the attack on the personal causes of homelessness. It is the institution most capable of teaching individuals the moral framework necessary to make good decisions and providing the social support system homeless people need to persevere.

[handwritten margin note: church & state combined]

Throughout the 1980s and into the present, the church and the state have offered incongruous responses to the homeless population. All too often, the two sides have been at odds, each calling upon the other to take responsibility and each abdicating leadership. (Obviously, those religious groups that reduce homelessness to a moral shortfalling do not offer a real response. Homeless people have been known to be "saved" several times each week to no avail.) At times, government has asked the religious community to bear the burden of response (Reagan's approach). Most often, however, the prophetic elements of the synagogues and churches have called for the government to do more. The result has been increased levels of funding for the McKinney Act and an on-again, off-again commitment from the religious community. This squabble—the church/state issue—prevented the response to homelessness from ever becoming a dialogue and has resulted in more homeless men, women, and children than America has experienced since the Great Depression.

With the inability to correctly identify the complex causes of homelessness and with no one taking a definitive role of leadership in response to the crisis, to whom can the thousands of men, women, and children who sleep on the streets every night look for hope and direction? The government responds to the homeless issue the way it responds to most problems—by throwing money at it (as pointed out by Jonathan Kozol in speeches after the release of his book *Rachel and Her Children*). At least this response has kept thousands of poor Americans alive and actually has enabled several hundred to overthrow (but never to forget) their homelessness. There have been too many restrictions applied to how McKinney funds are allocated, however, to allow the majority of the funds to go directly to the homeless. The majority of these funds, after intense lobbying efforts by government social service agencies, have ended up flowing through the agencies created by President Johnson's Great Society programs. Sadly, these agencies, after experiencing the cutbacks of the seventies and eighties, saw a new pot of funding in the McKinney Act and thus created new programs to access these monies, which revived their organizations. The result has been new social service bureaucracies that work with the homeless shelters and programs only to justify their new funding.

Nevertheless, the government's response has been better than that offered by the churches and synagogues. Religious organizations have been at a loss for what to do with biblical mandates to care for the poor, at least ever since they abdicated leadership during the Roosevelt administration. Certainly church resources were diminished during the Depression, but the religious community switched saviors all too quickly when they experienced the heat of poverty. Since that time, mainline churches and synagogues have not done well with their poorer members. Reflecting popular culture more than religious principles, they have sought to attract contributing members more than those who needed community the most. When President Kennedy called for the establishment of community mental health centers rather than insane asylums for the mentally ill and the NIMBY (not in my back yard) syndrome was born in neighborhoods across the country, religious institutions opted for consistent contributors. Rather than adhering to basic biblical principles, they kept silent while members led the fight to prevent the neighborhood mental health centers from opening. In the time since, the religious community has continued to adapt to popular culture by building family life centers with religious bowling alleys and televising their shows to those who find them bankrupt, always asking for money. Caring for the mentally ill or the homeless would prevent the church from doing the things that draw crowds, such as offering a bowling alley ministry, or from balancing their elaborate budgets by ministering to those who can afford to tithe. While there are numerous exceptions, the religious community as a whole has little concrete compassion for the poor, the sick, and the homeless.

Because of the vacuum created by this unwillingness of America's most significant institutions to take a role of leadership, today's homeless continue to be left outside. Unable to gain the power their numbers could command (3 million individuals constitute a powerful voting block) the homeless are noticed by politicians only when forced upon them. The homeless are viewed as just another unwanted social problem among many. They are unable to move the religious community's sense of compassion; the homeless would tax church and synagogue resources rather than augment them. The single most visible expression the church gives the homeless is locked doors.

Many will immediately point out the exceptions to this bleak situation. Government programs that make a difference will be cited. Congregations that have given and have gone above and beyond the call of duty will be raised up as illustrations that the religious community does care. The notion of compassion is not being questioned here. Most do not want to see anyone living on the streets. Government bureaucrats and religious leaders alike believe they are doing everything within their power to address the needs of the homeless. Despite heroic efforts on the part of many, however, there are more homeless men, women, and children each year. Regardless of the exceptions, most express their compassion only in the vaguest sense, and concern without action is not the stuff that makes for change.

Making this more frustrating is the fact that today's homeless want to be helped. The sad thing is that most have little idea of how to receive assistance. In *Giving and Taking Help*, Alan Keith-Lucas points out that helping establishes a reciprocal relationship.[4] One must offer assistance and another must choose to receive it. There is no question that thousands of individuals have sought to help today's homeless one time or another. Most of the help given is unstructured and ultimately ends up being meaningless and frustrating for the helper. Many well-intentioned individuals have entered into helping relationships with the homeless only to feel abused when golden opportunities they provide are ruined by bad decisions. Normally, the relationship abruptly ends when the helper can no longer stand the decisions or when the homeless fall under the weight of someone else's expectations. When the relationship endures, however, many homeless individuals overcome their situation.

Out of this vacuum a new mechanism is beginning to emerge for helping the homeless. Throughout the twentieth century, there have been shelters for the homeless. The majority were a response to yesterday's homeless population of winos, transients, or vagrants who chose their life style. That response viewed homelessness as a moral condition and, in most cases, offered an evangelical Christian response. Food and shelter were an excuse to address the "real" solution of "saving the lost." Those who received the shelter's services were required to attend evangelistic services. The Salvation Army and the Union Mission chain of shelters were built around this approach and, in many cases, conversions to the faith did help individuals overcome their homelessness. In fact, it could be argued that the homeless named their demons when they invited Jesus into their hearts. But the vast majority of the homeless in these shelters were "saved" several times each week for years to no avail.

When the characteristics of the homeless population changed, the shelters were slow to respond. Throughout the 1970s and early 1980s, the Salvation Army and Union Mission modified their response only slightly. Interventions began to include treatment for alcoholics and work-training programs. As the numbers seeking shelter escalated, these institutions were forced to take government funds to enhance their operations. In most shelters, religious services were no longer mandated, but the homeless were "strongly encouraged" to attend. As the numbers continued to grow, shelter programs could not keep up and began to resemble human warehouses, crowding as many people as possible inside. There was no time or space to offer any significant response to the problem. Even shelter chapels were turned into overflow sleeping areas.

In the mid-eighties, a new form of sheltering began to emerge that is different from those just described. Recognizing that basic food and shelter were not an answer to homelessness and desiring to do more than simply keep the homeless alive, these shelters began offering more in-depth intervention services and making use of government-funded services willing to locate in the shelter system. A basic assumption of these new shelters was that the homeless would take advantage of services if they were readily available. The more services in a shelter, the better chance the homeless would use them. Until then, most people who attempted to navigate the maze of the social service delivery system quickly frustrated at the hurry-up-and-wait mechanism in place. After several weeks of "securing services," many gave up and tried to make it on their own.

A play performed by a group of homeless men and women in Savannah for a group of local politicians makes this point. A man checks into a shelter, is given forms to complete, and is told that if he wishes to receive job training and placement to be at the Department of Labor office at 8:30 a.m. Leaving the shelter at 6:00 a.m., he walks several miles to the location. After waiting two hours, he is seen and it is discovered that he does not have the appropriate identification. The caseworker gives him forms to complete and tells him to return with a Social Security card. Leaving the office, he walks several miles to the Social Security office, where he takes a number and waits. He skips lunch so he does not lose his place in line. When he is seen, he is given another form to complete. As the play is performed, the homeless actor goes from one office to another, receives additional forms to complete, and finally cannot be seen for the stack of paper he is carrying. The skit ends when, in a fit of frustration, he throws the paper in the air. The new type of homeless shelter combines all of these services, making them available to the homeless on an outreach basis. Instead of asking the homeless to go to the services, the assistance is brought to them. This allows immediate help as it is needed. Case management in the shelters provides better coordination of services for each individual.

In addition, the comprehensive-services shelter demands accountability from the homeless. If the shelter is going to provide food, shelter, and other services, the homeless are expected to do whatever it takes to help themselves. The shelter helps the homeless help themselves. If the residents are not interested in helping themselves, then food and shelter are about the only things they will receive. Using Alan Keith-Lucas's definition, helping is a reciprocal relationship. If certain homeless people are not ready to be helped, the new type of shelter will only frustrate them. There are numerous shelters that still exist only to provide basic services, and these individuals will eventually find them. People who are not prepared to face their homelessness will naturally leave the new type of shelter. Those who choose homelessness will reside in the old shelters.

The approach of today's shelter is acknowledged when entering the facility. The operation seeks to combine compassion with a professional and businesslike approach. The staff does everything possible to prevent the shelter from looking like the stereotype people have of such places. The office area resembles those in normal business atmospheres and is clean and efficient. The necessary tools of today's business are available, such as copy machines, computers, fax machines, and file cabinets. A shelter is a business, after all, albeit a nonprofit one, and it should function as such. Just because the activity is compassion and generates no profit does not mean the shelter should function like anything other than what it is—a business with a certain set of values dealing with certain commodities. A professional attitude permeates the building. The kitchen is clean and efficient. The rest rooms sparkle. The floor of every room shines.

The same care is given to the exterior. The shelter fits into the neighborhood. Dirty men do not lie on the steps but busy themselves cleaning the yard. If the entire area is poor and run-down, the shelter sets an example and does what it can to upgrade the neighborhood. Flower beds and trees are planted. Fresh paint is constantly added (paint is one of the easiest things to get donated). One of the reasons the NIMBY syndrome exists is that shelters often *do* drag down the neighborhood. Outside and in, the shelter must provide an atmosphere that makes the homeless know how they are expected to act.

Of course, this raises the question of how a shelter's staff can get computers, keep floors shining, and upgrade the neighborhood when it is worried about where next week's meals are coming from. It starts easily enough. The shelter should be clean. An example must be set for the homeless and for the potential contributor. The cost of a clean shelter is not reflected in the budget or in the number of meals served. It does make a significant difference, however, in the attitude of the helper and the helped. Most shelters in America are overdue for an attitude adjustment. If the shelter looks like a junkyard, then most of the donations will be junk. Old clothes and broken-down typewriters are simply not acceptable. Each time a donation is received, regardless of how bad a contribution it may be, staff should take the opportunity to explain what the shelter should look like.

Eventually, the point will be made. Of course, some contributors will have a negative reaction to this, but the long-term effectiveness of the shelter is at stake. Those who care about the homeless will respond positively. Those who clean out their closets and bring donations only for the tax receipt are not worth worrying about.

The other important thing to notice about the emerging type of shelter is how the homeless themselves are partners in its development. Because most government funding is directed toward the newly-established homeless bureaucracies, shelters have been forced to develop without appropriate funding. When shelters are without funding for secretaries, the homeless learn how to answer phones, take messages, and address envelopes. When shelters choose to fund caseworkers rather than janitors, the homeless learn how to clean and maintain a building as well as any professional service. When shelters are without drivers to pick up needed donations, the homeless drive the shelter vehicle to the suburbs in order to load the donated materials. When there are no purchasing agents to choose what is needed from the food bank, the homeless have the skills necessary to determine which foodstuffs work best in a mass feeding. When statistics are needed, the homeless know (better than most) how to complete forms. Today's shelter creates a working partnership between the helper and the helped. The new shelter forces two worlds to collide, thereby helping both.

Certainly there are difficulties with such an approach. Bringing the homeless into the management of a shelter creates many problems. A great strain is placed on the "professional" employees to constantly train the homeless employees or the volunteers in addition to their normal duties. When a homeless person is trying to master answering a phone with four lines, hold buttons, transfer mechanisms, and intercom systems and the social worker is attempting to make phone referrals at the same time, it takes great patience and focus to train and retrain the homeless employee. If this were not enough, such an approach often leads to frustration on the part of the employee, the social worker, and the callers who are repeatedly cut off and must redial. The initial attempts to create such a partnership can certainly be taxing on all involved. Nevertheless, the end results are a less costly and more professional shelter, a homeless person with new marketable skills, and a community impressed with the approach. There will be times when the homeless refuse to cooperate, the social workers throw up their hands in frustration, and the callers become angry. The new shelter will remain focused on the end result, however, sticking to the partnership model.

Despite the success of these new shelters, it is apparent that the response to today's homeless population has not worked. Blame may be placed on the government, the religious organizations, the existing mechanisms of funding, the current social service system, and the homeless themselves. A new response must be developed that takes the best from the old ways, breaks down the barriers preventing a unified attack on homelessness, and creates a new partnership in which each institution is involved. It is not only the homeless who must learn to name their demons, but governments must recognize that throwing money at a problem is no answer and that many of the old funding mechanisms do not work in today's world. Religious organizations must regain their mission to be communities to all of society's members, especially the poor. The current social service system has to understand that it is fighting a losing war if it wins only funding battles. Yesterday's shelters have to know that they are making little difference meeting the true needs of the homeless. If new territory is not surveyed, the homeless problem will continue to worsen, and all parties will grow increasingly frustrated at their inability to make a significant difference. This new territory will be explored when all involved name their own demons and learn that recognition of a problem is half the solution.

THE HOMELESS POPULATION

When asked to identify who the homeless are, most people respond by offering a description of male alcoholics who push grocery carts around, panhandle money, and make themselves an unsightly nuisance in the community. Such perceptions were true (at least, as true as stereotypes can be) in years past but are no longer valid. Yesterday's homeless population does not mirror today's. All seem to agree, however, that there are more people on the streets now than at any time since the Great Depression. At one extreme, homeless advocates claim there are over 3 million homeless people in the United States. At the other, some studies report that the actual number is about .5 million. The 1990 census attempted a count but admitted from the beginning that their process was flawed. Exact figures are difficult to establish. As Mary Ellen Hombs and Mitch Snyder pointed out: "No one can say with any certainty how many people in this nation are homeless. Not until they come inside will we know for certain how many there are."[1]

While recent reports have claimed that the nation is over its "homeless slump,"[2] this has not proven to be the case. It is true that numerous emergency shelters and intervention programs were developed in the 1980s to assist the exploding homeless population. In the 1990s, these programs are operating at capacity or have downsized in an effort to go after quality rather than quantity. The numbers suggesting fewer homeless individuals are based on the number of people that shelters serve on a daily basis. These shelters are operating at capacity and have been for the past several years, so the number of homeless people served has naturally leveled off. The actual number of homeless is still unknown and will remain unknown until everyone has the opportunity to participate in these programs.

The faces of those living on the streets have changed. Gone are the hobos of the past. In his 1923 classic, *The Hobo*, Nels Anderson offers classifications of five types of homeless men: "(a) the seasonal worker, (b) the transient or occasional worker or hobo, (c) the tramp who 'dreams and wanders' and works only when it is convenient, (d) the bum who seldom wanders and seldom works, and (e) the home guard who lives in hobohemia and does not leave town."[3] The homeless of the 1920s were mostly men, white, and between thirty and sixty years old. Throughout most of this century, this portrait has been the norm. As late as the 1960s, says Deirdre Carmody in a *New York Times* article, "The typical person in a shelter was male, over fifty years old and alcoholic."[4]

During the 1980s, however, the homeless population began to include both sexes, grew younger, and included people of more racially diverse backgrounds. This redefinition of who was homeless displaced the old stereotype which is still prevalent. Today's homeless population is made up of young men and women who are not homeless by choice. They are from all educational backgrounds. All races are represented. They are angry and ill. Unless drastic change occurs, they will continue to grow in number. In the 1990s, the homeless population may be broken into three broad categories—children, women, and men. With the continued demise of the nuclear family in America, today's homeless represent the fallen branches of a broken family tree.

CHILDREN

Jonathan Kozol, in *Rachel and Her Children*, describes the change best. "What was once a theater of the grotesque (bag ladies . . . winos . . .) has grown into the common misery of millions."[5] In years past, the homeless population was mostly male, old, and intoxicated; this group is now only a subgroup of a broader homeless population. While the stereotype of the homeless has not changed, the population has. The new homeless are younger, male and female, and are usually not substance abusers when they first become homeless. The National Academy of Sciences estimates that 100,000 American children go to sleep homeless at night, and the Children's Defense Fund estimates that as many as 2 million American children are homeless every year. "The chilling fact, from any point of view," Kozol continues, "is that small children have become the fastest growing segment of the homeless. . . . The average homeless family includes two or three children. The average child is six years old, the average parent twenty-seven."

Regardless of the specific number, homeless children now constitute one-fourth to one-third of the nation's homeless population. Obvious questions come to mind. Why are so many of today's homeless population children? What are the social conditions that force them onto the streets of our communities? Given these social conditions, what should our response to homeless children be? The literature on homelessness has not had time to determine why so many children are on the streets of America. Most advocates assume it is for the same reasons adult men and women experience homelessness. While these reasons certainly contribute to families on the streets, another cause may be teenage pregnancy. This hypothesis uncovers what is believed by many to be a unique contribution to the root causes of homelessness. It is understandable that teenage pregnancy would lead to homelessness. "Teen parents do not fare as well in school. They are much less likely to complete school than those who defer parenting until they reach age twenty. The lifetime earnings of those who become parents as teens are much lower than those of other parents," explains an article by the Georgia Department of Human Resources and the Chatham-Savannah Youth Futures Authority.[6]

The current literature does not reflect teenage pregnancy as a contributing factor to homelessness. Most experts agree that people become homeless because of certain social factors. Too often, homeless advocates cease searching to understand the problem when they uncover reasons related to government policies. This is understandable. Social workers and advocates understand government policy and issues of funding. Most of their own salaries are government generated. When they realize that deinstitutionalization and cuts in federal housing contribute to the rise in homelessness, they immediately concentrate all of their energies on these policies. Unfortunately, these policies are only a part of the reason.

Teenage pregnancy as a contributing factor to the rise of homeless families with children makes a *direct* impact on the parents' ability to raise their children and an *indirect* impact on the children's ability to maximize their opportunities. For homeless parents, it takes approximately four years from the time of their first child until they enter the shelter system. Given the federal definition of homelessness as being without a regular or fixed address (according to the Stewart B. McKinney Act of 1987), most parents likely experience homelessness earlier, but do not enter a shelter immediately. Homeless parents spend months moving from one relative or friend to another with their children in tow. During the intervening years, the parents descend the social ladder in the following sequence:

1. They live with their own parents after the first child's birth until they are forced to leave due to overcrowding or the fact that their parents are living in public housing and cannot have guests for more than two weeks.

2. They move in with "friends" or enter into a significant social relationship in an attempt to "make it on their own." A second child is often conceived at this time.

3. They move back in with their parents, or the children move in with their grandparents while the parents continue trying to "make it on their own."

4. They enter the shelter system and attempt to regain responsibility for their "family."

In my experience, the grandparents of homeless children most often take the lead in shelter placement. Simply put, a grandparent tells or forces, by taking away other options, his or her son or daughter to take the grandchildren and move to a shelter. In some cases, when a shelter resident is in danger of being forced to leave because of a failure to comply with rules, his or her mother or father will visit the shelter and intervene on the children's behalf. Most homeless parents show little ability to manage their own affairs without the guidance of a strong advocate. Histories of instability explain why homeless men and women have so much trouble establishing themselves as independent adults.

One recent study stresses how homelessness affects a family: "Homelessness disrupts virtually every aspect of family life. It is a devastating experience for children and parents alike, damaging their physical and emotional health, interfering with their children's education and development, and resulting too often in the separation of family members."[7] Given the stress of homelessness and the lack of direction from the parents, it is not surprising that the children exhibit a wide range of psychological, social, and cognitive problems. Bassuk, Laruiat, and Rubin report that "homeless children . . . [have] difficulty not only with language skills but in fine and gross motor skills and social and personal development as well. In the school-age children, almost half were extremely depressed and anxious."[8]

The National Commission on Children adds that "failure

to prevent childhood poverty and address the economic needs of families leads to other social ills—more crime and delinquency, more teenage childbearing, more unhealthy babies, more failure in school, more substance abuse and mental illness, more child abuse and neglect, and lower productivity by tomorrow's labor force."[9]

When a family enters a shelter, the children should be required to attend school as quickly as possible. The local board of education should be helpful in making school accessible to the children. However, attending school presents special challenges to homeless kids. Because the children are so transient, it is difficult to keep track of school records and register them properly. Local boards of education have been especially helpful in this regard, many times, overlooking the lack of records and enrolling the children in school immediately. It is also important to note that school-age homeless children have the right to attend their school of origin and must be provided the transportation to get there (according to the McKinney Act). While the school will often allow the children to attend, there may be little cooperation when the appropriate documentation is not in place. Advocates can sometimes do their best work at this level. Homeless parents are often more concerned with securing immediate food and shelter than with maintaining the necessary records. Often the homeless family is in a constant state of emotional crisis, and educational issues become a low priority. Inevitably, the children pick up on the emotional distress of their parents. When they *do* attend school, they are depressed, anxious, and distracted. Learning is almost impossible. The shelter system must take the lead in intervening for the children as soon as possible because the parents likely do not have the capacity to take full responsibility for the educational needs of their children.

Homeless children need special educational help. They need an appropriate learning environment at "home," even in a homeless shelter. The immediate solution seems simple—provide volunteers who will act as tutors to assist

[handwritten margin note: homeless children immediately in school]

the children with homework. Sadly, volunteers often prove to be inconsistent in their methods and attitudes, helping in an effort to meet their own needs rather than those of the children. To be effective, tutors must understand and appreciate the children's homelessness for real learning to occur, and homeless parents must understand that they must learn how to help their children learn. This is where an after-school program can help to teach parents these important lessons. Young homeless children who participate in a program that augments their education become genuinely enthused and more productive students.

Most importantly, homeless parents who see educational programs at work want their children to succeed. Too often, these parents are stereotyped by their homelessness and—because of their socioeconomic condition—are perceived as not caring about their children's future. On the contrary, most homeless parents know that education is the key to their children's ability to avoid repeating the pattern of homelessness. There are exceptions, but rarely do shelter staffs encounter homeless parents who do not support augmented educational programs once the programs are explained.

Homeless parents often do not know how to help their children meet educational goals. Many homeless parents were still in school when they had their first child. They dropped out and never learned how to be a healthy student. Consequently, they do not know how to teach their children to learn. The shelter must be prepared to train the parents in this regard. This is best accomplished when a member of the shelter staff and an educator meet with the parents to explain how to meet the children's educational needs. Such meetings help the parents learn to create an appropriate environment for their children's education. The shelter staff then stresses the importance of allowing a snack when the children first come home from school, providing some recreational activities after school, and then completing all homework assignments. This after-school routine is parallel to that of children who are not homeless.

The parents thus learn the importance the shelter places on their children's education. A sense of partnership between all involved guarantees that the lessons learned by the parents will be taken with them when they exit the shelter.

There must be clear lines of communication between the school and the shelter at all times. Once communicated, most problems are easily corrected. When a shelter first begins placing homeless children in public schools, the local board of education is often slow to respond to the needs of this special population. The shelter's agenda is to keep the children in their school of origin since they have already experienced the drastic move from a home to homelessness. It is not uncommon for homeless children to attend as many as four different schools in three months. The local transportation department's standard operating procedure, which calls for certain districts to be transported to certain schools, sometimes makes it difficult to keep children in their school of origin, even though the McKinney Act mandates it. With appropriate intervention by the parents and the staff, the board of education must identify the process by which homeless children can remain in their school of origin.

When a family arrives at the shelter, the parents must go to the board of education and show that they are concerned about their children's education in spite of their homelessness. The student is immediately placed in the appropriate school and the shelter staff can then call the transportation department and confirm the transportation. On the same trip, the parent goes to the local department of health to obtain or transfer necessary school records. Parents new to the state receive an immediate transfer of state records, which allows their children to be in school the next day.

After-school programs must be developed to augment the children's educational experience after their school day. This is extremely important as it enables the children to appreciate their education and to learn that the single most important need for them is not to experience homelessness when they are older. These programs seek to enhance homeless children's chances of being successful in school by establishing a stable "home" environment in the shelter. Even with a stable and structured environment, the key is individual tutoring. The program is effective because the children receive individual support and encouragement.

After-school programs located in the shelter have proven to be very successful. I recall Penny, a ten-year-old resident of a shelter, asking every day, "Can we start the program now? Is the teacher going to be here? What are we going to do today?" Similar excitement is expressed by all of the children. When children share their report cards—noting with pleasure and enthusiasm the rise in their grades—it is apparent that they have taken hold of the key that may unlock their futures and lead them out of homelessness, hopefully never to return.

The strong bonding among the children in after-school programs has been an unexpected benefit. Differences in age, race, or gender have not deterred the development of close friendships. During self-esteem and problem-solving sessions, peers are quick to support children experiencing difficulties. Homeless children are not only sensitive but appear to know the right thing to say to make another child feel better. The older children help younger children with special needs that only someone who has experienced homelessness can understand. In essence, the children become a family.

There is an obvious sense of sorrow and loss when a child moves from the shelter into a home. Promises to visit or stay in touch are often exchanged between the children during these times. The sadness expressed by children remaining in the shelter when one of their peers is moving out is extreme. Considering their diverse backgrounds, these relationships become a key component of the program. When Mason—who is black—left the shelter, Laura—who is white—was obviously upset and heartsick. "When are we going to get some more kids in here?" Laura asked.

Interaction with peers and adults not living at the shelter

is a valuable resource for homeless children. Positive role models permit the children to temporarily forget they are different, insecure, and homeless. Surprisingly, children who are not homeless visiting the shelter have no difficulty relating to or interacting with children residing in the shelter. Likewise, homeless children show little concern when they interact with someone who is not homeless.

Volunteers are often inconsistent in their teaching and, therefore, do not provide the same quality of experience from day to day. An organized orientation for select and regular volunteers encourages more effective, dedicated role models. However, it takes volunteers to train volunteers. There are rarely enough helpers. School supplies, snacks, and clothing are always in short supply. The population of the shelter itself changes with the particular population of families currently in-house. Planned shelter activities, changes in staff responsibilities, and changes in shelter rules are always occurring. In short, it is extremely difficult to obtain a level of consistency in an inconsistent setting. A retired school principal stated in a requested critique of one after-school program that it seemed impossible to achieve anything, considering the age range of the children. It is only through participation, the principal added, that one can see that the program is not only possible but vital to the children.

Numerous problems emerge from the families themselves. A close working relationship between teachers and the shelter staff to remain focused on what is best for the children is essential. The shelter staff, overwhelmed by responding to continuous need, can provide only minimal support for the program. Contact with the local school system regarding the problems of homeless children must be frequent and uncomplicated. The few teachers, bus drivers, and other who are sympathetic, understanding, and supportive of homeless children would be amazed at the difference they are making in these children's lives.

The need is growing rapidly for additional self-help programs for children in the areas of street safety, sexual and physical abuse, substance abuse, health and dental care, and self-esteem development. Children should leave the shelter feeling better about themselves and knowing that, with continued hard work, they will succeed in school, thus increasing their chances for success later in life. Likewise, it is beneficial for additional intervention programs to have the necessary funds to hire a full-time coordinator. A major part of the success of the program is the security the children have of knowing, and liking, the person who greets them after school each afternoon. A great deal of the children's commitment is not so much to the program as it is to someone who cares about them.

Our communities must face the fact that children now constitute one-fourth to one-third of America's homeless population. With the changes in the makeup of the homeless population, it is important to note that most communities' perceptions have not altered. When asked, most citizens will still say that the homeless population is comprised mostly of men who do not work and who are substance abusers. While it is easy to take a "pull yourself up by your own bootstraps" attitude with adults, such attitudes do not apply to children. Homeless children are the innocent victims of society's inability to deal with significant social problems.

It is amazing to staff and volunteers that homeless children, despite their circumstances, maintain a sense of confidence in their future. For them, the future is full of possibilities not yet made inaccessible by societal barriers. Sadly, while homeless children express a strong desire to learn (once shown how to combine recreation with education), there simply is not enough organized response to their need. Until our communities provide the necessary understanding, compassion, and resources to help homeless children, these children will continue to grow in number and, in all likelihood, will eventually follow in their parents' footsteps.

WOMEN

While various people estimate that children make up one-fourth to one-third of the homeless population, women are thought to at least equal that proportion. It is difficult to blame children for their homelessness; it is also difficult to understand how single women live on the streets. Single homeless women have perhaps the most difficult experience of all the subpopulations who live outside. Compared to families and other groups, single women are small in number; thus the large number of single homeless women suggests that they move in and out of homelessness with higher rates of frequency than any other component of the population.

Single women are the greatest survivors of homelessness. To be a single woman on the streets is to live in constant fear and danger. They are targets of rape. Living with their guard up at all times, the mental health of single women becomes a matter of concern. Psychiatrists have documented that one-fourth of the homeless are mentally ill. This is widely accepted by advocates, yet it is difficult to determine if these individuals are homeless because they are mentally ill or if they experience mental illness because of the stress of their homelessness. Certainly, both cases occur.

For single women, however, mental health problems become pronounced after only a short period of time. While other issues related to homelessness exist for single women, they do not appear to be as significant as the issue of mental health. Single women do not seem to know how to navigate the social service maze, and because many shelters concentrate on homeless families, these women are often neglected. In addition, government funding does not address the needs of single women as it does those of families. In spite of the danger of the streets, the lack of available services, and the increased tendencies for mental health problems, women learn to cope with homelessness in three primary ways: through sexual favors and substance abuse, by denying their condition, or by trying to ignore their situation.

Some single women use the desire some men have for them to their advantage. Sexual favors and intimacy are exchanged for the promise of housing and a permanent mate. Typically young and often, but not always, addicted, these women attach themselves to a man for protection. Many are abused by these men. They are forced to have sex on demand, or they use sex to obtain drugs.

Again, it is difficult to determine which comes first: the homelessness or the addiction. Using sexual favors to survive homelessness is often a short-term solution because the life of a crack prostitute or the never-ending search for a better man to offer protection are both extremely dangerous. Once women engage these coping mechanisms, they are extremely difficult—many would argue impossible—to help. Such women are not regulars in the shelter system, as they are easily prone to violence and disruption. Simply put, they are usually barred from the shelter before any intervention has an opportunity to work. Most pass their lives outside, hustling for a man or for themselves. The majority do not live long enough to have a second chance.

Other women become so disoriented that they aimlessly wander the streets, screaming graphic insults at anyone who invades their space. Many of these women are displaced homemakers who have divorced and have not worked in years. Reluctant to enter the shelters, they deny their demons, refusing to admit their homelessness. Bag ladies load their possessions in grocery carts or in knapsacks, shuffling their feet from one end of their area to another. Most are antisocial personalities who long ago developed pronounced mental health problems and have simply learned to live alone with them. They have little or no concept of time, something easily lost on the streets, and they eat when they are hungry and relieve themselves when they must. Having convinced themselves that there is

reminds me of nature obsessors

no need for social interactions with others, these women sleep in doorways or abandoned houses until they die from the exhaustion of keeping everyone else at bay.

Some say that most people choose to deal with their problems by ignoring them. This is the case with women who choose to cope with their homelessness by ignoring it. Seeking to maintain some degree of dignity, they visit beauty shops for free samples and spend countless hours rummaging through clothing closets to find the most acceptable second-hand wear. Also slow to trust, these women look for the best opportunities to help themselves, tracking down numerous job leads or volunteering in the shelter in the hope that something will work out. Out of these are the few who climb out of their homelessness. Such an experience leaves them scared and doubtful, but these women are the greatest survivors of homelessness.

Certainly there are exceptions to these three classifications, but they are in the minority. While these descriptions are only brief sketches of the types of single women who experience homelessness, those who work with or for them see all these types on a daily basis. Nevertheless, these homeless women are seldom discussed or reported on. They rarely come inside. Most are met outside the shelter. Offers of kindness may be accepted, but relationships are rarely formed. It is this lack of significant social relationships that keeps most women, indeed most people, homeless. The lack of an appropriate social support system is the single greatest contributing factor to homelessness.

When most Americans are out of work or experiencing difficult circumstances that could lead to downward mobility, it is their social support system that prevents disaster from occurring. Fathers and mothers help sons and daughters with money. Friends intervene with job leads. While many claim they are self-made men and women, this is never the case. There are always a host of helpful supporters in the background. Perhaps more important than these tangible expressions are the other ways people offer support. A husband who has been laid off and is spending his days going from one fruitless job interview to another comes home to a wife who pats him on the back, offers words of understanding and encouragement, and tells him tomorrow will be a better day. Friends express compassion and offer advice. Some lend money. More often, they become part of an informal network that leads the man to the company where he is eventually employed. While he may choose to believe that he finally found a job, that he endured the bad times, there was in fact a strong support system sustaining him, supporting him, and guiding him to the new position. The homeless have no such system.

This lack is most easily seen when homeless people eat. In soup kitchens and shelters across the country, the scene is repeated daily. When most of us eat, we do so as part of our social support system. At a common table, with family or friends, we communicate while we eat. Because of this, it takes a while to complete the meal. Even for those individuals who prefer solitude, the most memorable meals are those that include good food, good friends, and good conversation. Among the homeless, there is bland food prepared for the masses, tables full of strangers, and no conversation. It takes approximately ten minutes for one hundred people to eat a meal and line up for seconds. There is little social interaction of any kind. Without the necessary support systems in place—and with few programs designed to foster such relationships—women have little chance of leaving the streets permanently. Again, what keeps most homeless people on the streets is the lack of significant social support systems. The majority of responses to homelessness to date have not taken this important factor into account, and until the delivery system incorporates personal relationships into social services, homelessness will continue on its current course.

Making contact and establishing relationships with homeless people is the challenge of those attempting to incorporate the development of social support systems into the current delivery system. "This engagement process begins by nonintrusive offering of basic services (e.g., food,

[handwritten margin note: Build Homeless community, not simply shelters.]

shelter)."[10] Food and shelter become the beginning point of relationship building with the homeless. It is important to note that basic food and shelter are *only* the beginning points. The government is beginning to note this fact by placing funding emphasis on interventions (e.g., job training, education, and so forth) rather than on basic services. Service providers are following this lead by downsizing shelters and building their programs around these interventions. It appears that the new emphasis will be quality of service instead of quantity of those served.

Certainly, a major portion of providers' motivation is to follow the money and maintain their programs, but there is the emerging recognition that past efforts have not been successful. Until providers fully accept that a key component of eradicating homelessness is the development of social support systems and then build their major programs with this concept in mind, services to the homeless will continue to be aimed at the conditions that create homelessness but not at the principle reason that it exists and continues.

Providers can recount numerous "success" stories of finding someone a job, securing housing, and moving the individual out of homelessness back into society, only to have the person reappear several months later at the shelter. When this occurs, the need for follow-up case management is typically cited as the reason for failure. What actually happens, however, is that there is no social support system to rely on when key choices are made. In most cases, the shelter staff becomes the person's primary support system. Once the individual is out on his or her own, alone, old patterns repeat themselves. When this occurs— after the job is in jeopardy or lost, or one is evicted—the person naturally returns to the last set of significant others available to him or her: the shelter staff. In the end, people are homeless because they are alone and, when left to their own devices, they often make poor decisions when placed in an unhealthy environment. Bag ladies are perhaps the best visual image of what happens to someone totally and completely alone.

MEN

American culture expects men to make it on their own, relying on no one, as though they have some inherent ability to pull themselves up by their own bootstraps regardless of any situation. Americans champion the images of those who succeed alone, often against impossible odds. Nothing is further from the truth, of course, and thousands of men cannot possibly live an American Dream that is little more than pure fantasy.

Men make up the largest group in today's homeless population. At first look, homeless men appear to be white alcoholics or black drug users. They are viewed as unsightly, bad-smelling panhandlers who urinate in public places, and have no desire to work. When most Americans think about the homeless, this is the image that pops into their minds first; this dirty, smelly, and often obscene version of Charlie Chaplin does not invoke compassion. The result is that as the public and private sectors have responded to the needs of the homeless in the 1980s, the majority of resources have been directed toward women and especially toward children. With some exceptions, men have been left to fend for themselves.

Yet they are not simply a mass of men. Even to identify them according to subclassification—veterans, employed, unemployed, mentally ill, and so on—loses sight of who these men are: the father and husband of a family living in our antifamily welfare system (where the assumption is that if the man is in the home then he should be working, and there is no need for public assistance) who leaves his family so the state will put food on the table and provide them with medicine when the children are sick; the mentally ill brother whose parents are long dead and whose siblings are much too busy with their own lives to care for him

now that the state, through the policy of deinstitutionalization, leaves him to wander through the mental health system bouncing between shelters and state hospitals; the son
proud enough to make it on his own without asking anyone, even his parents, for help, working day-labor jobs with
little thought of anything other than finding work tomorrow.

These men are fathers, sons, brothers, and lost friends.
Most do not wander far from home, choosing to gravitate to
the nearest city with a service delivery system. It is no
wonder then, when the television cameras turn their lights
on in a shelter, that the homeless turn their backs and howl
in protest. Only the mentally ill and the transient grant
interviews. The majority do not want their family and
friends to see them as they are now.

What happened to these homeless men, leading them
away from their families and friends and onto the streets?
In general, Americans would like to deal with the problem
of homeless men by ignoring them, but there are too many
cracks in the American Dream which allow too many men
to fall through to ignore. Many Americans also blame the
victim, so homeless men are deemed solely responsible for
their lot in life. Conservatives stop here, while liberals
blame the systemic factors that create homelessness. From
an insider's point of view, both groups are right, and one is
no more right than the other. Liberals are correct in pointing to the loss of affordable housing, deinstitutionalization,
changes in the family structure, cutbacks in support programs, and growing poverty; these are major contributors
to the growing homeless population. Conservatives are not
right to blame the victim so much, but they are correct in
holding the homeless accountable to make good decisions
when opportunities are presented to them. But if homeless
men do not have significant support systems in place—and
they do not—there is no one to hold them accountable.
Without a sense of accountability, homeless men are left to
choose aimlessly, with no foundation for their decision
making, and most never overcome their life on the streets.

Those who do leave the shelters and become productive members of society again find new support systems to help them accomplish these things. For the homeless, there are no accomplishments without accountability, and there cannot be accountability without social support systems.

Accountability is a major key to helping homeless men and to understanding why they are homeless in the first place. It is not the only key, of course, but once someone is on the streets, it becomes the appropriate area to focus on. This is often forgotten by those who work with the homeless, who try to hold the government or the church accountable but forget the individuals they are interacting with daily. Understandably, it is a tough enough job to place food on the table and to provide clean, safe bedding for the homeless without also having to engage in a personal relationship with them. Resources always appear to be diminishing, fund-raising occupies too much time, volunteer training becomes a constant distraction, and countless men ask for assistance, making it virtually impossible for service providers to consider other courses of action. But until the development of social support systems is made the heart of helping the homeless, the problem will not significantly change. Even if there is ample housing, without support systems in place to foster the accountability needed to maintain these units, men will still be homeless.

While the most basic needs of homeless men are food and shelter, the most important intervention may be a new sense of family to replace the one no longer available. Offering basic services will bring the homeless to the shelter, but the real work begins afterward. To break the cycle of homelessness for men, someone must sit down with each one individually and ask him what it is he wants for himself. The answers are already apparent—men will cite jobs, housing, health care, mental health care, transportation, relocation of their families, and so on. After identifying these needs, the service provider facilitates the process of prioritizing them. Priority one is a job. Priority two is obtaining safe and affordable housing. Priority three is relocating the family to the new home. These goals and objectives are written down, creating a record.

At this point, the most critical portion of assistance is engaged. The goals and objectives are presented to the homeless individual as a contract. If the individual will sign the contract, pledging to work toward obtaining each of his own identified goals, then the service provider's job is to hold him accountable. So long as the individual works to obtain the things he has identified as most important, basic food, shelter, and support services are made available.

A time line is identified to which both agree, making it difficult for the homeless individual to abuse or manipulate the contract. Such a process provides an established entry to a confusing social service system and begins to lay the foundation for the social support system. Once this is in place, accountability drives the individual to meet his own goals. As long as the service provider functions appropriately, checking daily with the individual, pointing him in the right directions, maintaining the time line, providing basic services, and not allowing the individual to get sidetracked, the prospect for success is maximized. The only way the process can falter is if either party fails to live up to its part of the contract; this failure means that the service provider is no longer keeping the best interest of the homeless individual at heart or the individual has sabotaged his own contract and forsaken his own goals.

The assumption here is, of course, that the man no longer desires to be homeless. Those who choose the life-style are quickly identified through the signing of the contract. As there have always been homeless people in America, such as those Nels Anderson identified earlier in this chapter, there likely will continue to be. This is the America where people are free to choose any life-style they wish; if someone wants to be homeless, he has the freedom to do so. A helping relationship will not be of much concern to those who wish to remain homeless. There will always be shelters that, for either humanitarian or religious reasons, offer basic food and shelter to those requesting these things, no questions asked. Those who are homeless and are not choosing that life-style, however, deserve the opportunity to leave the streets. The contract process allows for the identification of those who are not choosing homelessness and provides the foundation of one resource person, or friend, who will function as a primary support system.

Throughout the helping process, other key people are brought into the support system. The individual learns, or relearns, the process of socialization under the watchful eye of the service provider, who makes necessary referrals, gauges social interaction, and enforces the terms of the contract. As progress is made, the individual gains confidence and begins to assume more responsibility for his own actions. He will grow increasingly comfortable with social interactions and learn which kind of people he should build relationships with. The closer to the end of the time line, the stronger the individual becomes.

There are several critical junctures that should be kept in mind. The first is the signing of the contract with the homeless individual. This may be the first time for the homeless man that someone is perceived to care enough to sign the dotted line of an agreement that outlines a relationship. The agreement is presented as a marriage contract or a church covenant, placing the emphasis on the relationship. Simply put, the point of the paperwork is agreeing to be friends. As the service provider continues to broker services and the individual embraces, perhaps for the first time, what he really wants, they do so as partners. Without a personal investment by the provider, the contract is little more than a rehash of the provider's job description.

Second, there must be a transfer of the support system as the man gains confidence and experiences initial success. Other key people must be given credit for any progress made. The man should not become convinced that the provider is his only friend. From the moment the contract is signed, the provider begins preparing the man to learn to choose friends wisely and maintain relationships on his own. The man's long-term benefit is always to be kept in mind. Otherwise, the relationship will become narrow and unhealthy, setting the individual up to be overly dependent on one person. Such a relationship helps no one.

Third, the service provider must maintain clearly defined boundaries of helping that are always respected. While the relationship is a personal one, it cannot allow for shortcuts. The provider must be accessible without allowing all his or her time to be manipulated by one client. He or she must be a professional resource without making more personal investments than the relationship calls for. The provider must strike an appropriate balance between professional helper and friend without becoming a professional friend, one who is paid to be a friend of the homeless.

If the problem of homelessness is going to be successfully addressed, the methods used to date will not be enough. Food, shelter, and basic services have not made a significant dent in the number of homeless. New and creative interventions, as basic as food and shelter, must be used by those helping the homeless. The human need for a significant support system—a family—must be taken into account when one seeks to help the homeless. Relationships must be forged that do not shy away from holding the homeless accountable to help themselves. Most homeless individuals are open to such relationships and will engage in them when the opportunity presents itself. Service providers are willing to become support systems for the homeless. Many already have, but in an informal and unstructured way. Social workers, ministers, and volunteers do what they do because they want to make a difference in the lives of the homeless.

Thus both the homeless and the service providers are ready to enter into relationships, but such relationships are not developing. Why? Primarily because the government response to the homeless problem has become a major barrier, and the role of the church, save for some exceptions, has been diminished to token expressions of concern for "these the least of my brothers and sisters."

THREE

THE GOVERNMENT RESPONSE: THROWING MONEY AT THE PROBLEM

During the 1980s, government involvement with the homeless problem underwent a steady increase. By the later part of the decade, in 1987, the federal government had passed the Stewart B. McKinney Homeless Assistance Act to address the multifaceted problems of the homeless with a wide range of shelter programs that cut across federal agency boundaries. The Family Support Act of 1988 increased job training, education, and child-care opportunities for recipients of Aid to Families with Dependent Children (AFDC). In 1990, the National Affordable Housing Act created the HOME housing partnership grant program to generate needed housing units for the homeless. In addition, state governments established coalitions, task forces, and other funding sources to address these needs. At the same time, there was also a steady increase in the number of homeless people. "This apparent contradiction," writes Catherine Zudak, "shows every evidence of continuing in the 1990s, despite the efforts of private, non-profit, and governmental agencies."[1]

What happened? "'Let's face it,'" states Richard Kreimer, a homeless person, "'most of the current system is set up to perpetuate itself. It doesn't work.'"[2] If the homeless themselves recognize the well-intentioned but often misdirected help of the government, then certainly something is wrong with the system.

The problems began immediately. When the McKinney Act was conceived and debated in Congress, it was determined that existing funding mechanisms would be used to distribute the funds. Instead of reinventing the wheel, Congress sought to use programs it already funded to address the needs of the homeless. Advocates and lobbyists made certain that Congress was convinced that these agencies were the appropriate mechanism for delivering services. In reality, there was no real alternative to such a proposal at the time. Local responses to the homeless were in their infancy, or established organizations, like the Salvation Army, were prohibited from using federal funds because of religious restrictions. While the existing programs, community action agencies, and community mental health hospitals had not been established to meet the specific needs of the homeless, they did have experience with combating poverty. On a superficial level, such a move made sense.

As the first major source of new social service monies established by the federal government since the 1960s War on Poverty, agencies that had suffered diminishing budgets for fifteen years saw the opportunity for new revenue when the McKinney Act was passed. The lobbyists employed by these agencies did their job by restricting most of the funds to agencies that already existed. At the local level, few of the agencies had programs dedicated specifically to helping the homeless. To access the funds so desperately needed, they began to conceive and then implement such programs.

It is important to note the struggles these agencies had been through since the War on Poverty had ended. Their budgets had diminished annually, and in face of increasing need they had continued their battles with the evils of society. In applying for these new funds, agencies would create new programs toward which they could charge administrative fees. (Administrative fees are a percentage of a grant that the organization may charge to implement a program.) This was new money for organizations as poor as the people they sought to help.

By and large, these agencies did have experience working with other aspects of poverty, but not with the homeless. There was no acknowledgment of the fact that, while homelessness certainly denotes poverty, it is the most radical form of poverty, different from what agencies had experience with. Faced with a lack of funding alternatives, these committed organizations had little choice. New programs were created in order to be eligible for the funding. This is not to say that the individuals who worked for these organizations did not want to help the homeless. Most had given their lives to low-paying jobs that fought poverty. From the point of view of an institution slowly starving to death, however, the passage of the McKinney Act meant a chance for new life.

Unfortunately, the government did *not* choose those agencies that did have experience with the homeless. Shelters were ignored for two primary reasons. First, the majority were religious in nature or had been started by a congregation, and government regulations prevented the funding of such agencies. Second, shelters were independent in nature, largely funded by the private sector, and were viewed as second class when compared to organizations previously sanctioned by the government. Shelters were not part of the accredited social service system previously established. By choosing to fund only agencies that already relied heavily on their funding, the government opted to support those agencies they could control. Any businessperson realizes that it is bad business to invest in a company with no proven track record, yet this is precisely what happened with McKinney funds.

Another factor in the government's choice not to fund shelters lay with the perception of those who worked with the homeless. Many shelter employees had been vocal advocates at the local, state, and federal levels, calling for the federal government to get involved in the first place, and they were viewed as radicals. No one better illustrates this point than Mitch Snyder, whose role in the development of America's response to the homeless cannot be overestimated. Wearing an old army field jacket, and having a slightly unkempt appearance, Snyder typified for the nation what homeless advocates were. In spite of the way he chose to portray himself, Snyder was the first person to call national attention to homelessness and keep that attention focused until there was a response.

In many ways, he was a contradiction. Portraying himself as antiestablishment and antigovernment, he sought to hold the business community and the government responsible for homelessness and demanded they take action to correct the problem. Claiming he could not allow tax deductions for people who wanted to contribute to his shelter, he successfully fought for tax dollars to be allocated to fund social programs that would benefit the homeless. Suggesting he spoke for all who cared about the homeless, he often charged an appearance fee to homeless advocates in other parts of the country when invited to speak and applied the income to his own shelter operation. In spite of these contradictions, he was relentless in appealing to the nation to respond to the plight of homeless men, women, and children.

A master at public relations, he kept the tragedy of homelessness in the public eye. From carrying the ashes of deceased homeless people into congressional hearings to staging celebrity-studded marches demanding "Housing Now," he commanded the press in ways few others have. When outrageous antics would not work, he would place his own life on the line and fast, until the point of death, to maintain public pressure on the government.

In the tradition of Martin Luther King, Jr., and Malcolm X, both of whom were represented in Mitch Snyder's personality, he forced President Reagan, also a master of the media, to authorize funds for the homeless. In virtually every head-to-head battle the two had in the media, Snyder won. During those years he was perhaps the only person in America to out-Reagan the president. Almost single-handedly, Snyder and his coworkers forced the United States to face a social problem it would just as soon ignore.

While his antics worked at one level, they failed on another—they convinced the government that Snyder and people like him, shelter directors and other outspoken advocates, could not work within the system. Snyder spoke out for the homeless and against those who expressed little concern for them. When people would not listen, he did whatever it took to make them hear. This approach can be grating. Frederick Buechner writes, "There is no evidence to suggest that anyone ever asked a prophet home for supper more than once."[3] Toward the end of his life, Snyder alienated many people. Working on the premise that the squeaky wheel always gets the grease, he was too hard on others, never allowing room for compromise, and only giving the benefit of the doubt to the homeless themselves, taking each small success without any expression of gratitude, and continuing to call for the system and for individuals to move faster than they could or wanted to.

In the last days of his life he was portrayed as a humorless, ungrateful, and unrelenting demagogue. Conservative radio and television commentators made fun of him and the cause of the homeless. The "liberal" media grew weary of his methods and ignored him. Had Snyder paused to thank the nation for its response, however minimal he thought it was, he likely would have won over more people. Had he showed the ability to laugh at himself in the public eye, perhaps he could have endeared himself to others. Because he seemed to know only one way to speak for the homeless, he burst on the scene at the right time in a great flame, only to burn out before his time. Everyone who works with the homeless has felt a loss since his suicide.

From the time of his death, there has been no one national spokesperson for the homeless. The wheels set in motion by the McKinney Act, however, have continued to roll, and shelters—those most experienced in working with the homeless—have benefitted indirectly at best from these resources. The government works on the assumption that shelters do not know how to do anything other than provide the most basic services. While it is true that the majority of shelters do not have the resources necessary to provide more than basic food and shelter, they know from experience what will best help the homeless help themselves. Other agencies are still going through the trial-and-error method of discovering what works best. This approach is a waste of time for people dying on the streets and a poor use of the nation's resources.

As discussed, the government used existing funding mechanisms to allocate McKinney funds. The McKinney Act also called for the establishment of an Interagency Council on the Homeless to use public resources and programs in a more coordinated manner and to provide funds for programs aimed solely at the homeless. The establishment of the Interagency Council had merit; it made sense to mobilize all existing resources, coordinated under one umbrella, to begin the fight. It was also feasible to use existing agencies as the backbone of a response. To the government's credit, shelters were helped through emergency grants, which sought to get the homeless off the streets. Thus the theory behind the McKinney Act had few flaws; the implementation, however, left much to be desired.

Community action agencies, created in the 1960s, were slated to be one of the government-sanctioned mechanisms of funding. Originally developed as community-based organizations that combined professional social workers with poor citizens from local communities, these agencies were charged with empowering the poor to overcome their poverty. Neighborhoods were organized so that, with professional help, they could rehabilitate houses, reform schools, clean up vacant lots, and take charge of their homes. The funds did not last, however, although the agencies did. Through some miracle, they hung on despite budget cuts and hostile presidents.

Mental health agencies had been the 1960s answer to the problems of the mentally ill. During those years, reformers concluded that institutionalization in insane asylums was not an appropriate way to help the mentally ill, and a new approach was implemented. The policy of deinstitutionalization had two components. First, the asylums were to be closed. By and large, this was accomplished; most people acknowledged that these facilities were cruel and inhuman places that did little more than hide the problem.

Second, the mentally ill were to be placed into the community. It had been demonstrated that many mentally ill individuals placed in normal environments would get better. The benefits of new drugs helped to facilitate this process. The problem was that *normal environments* meant typical American neighborhoods. The plan called for small group homes, of eight to ten people, to open across the country. Unfortunately, this portion of the plan ran into immediate difficulty. As soon as word spread that a group home was to be opened in a neighborhood, residents formed coalitions to prevent the establishment of the facility. Citing potential decreases in their property values and fear of the mentally ill, residents claimed they were for the creation of small group homes, but not in their neighborhood. Such reaction has become so common it is now dubbed the NIMBY (not in my back yard) Syndrome. As a result, few of the group homes actually opened, and the newly released mentally ill eventually found themselves homeless. The majority of mental health interventions became outpatient in nature.

The government response to the housing needs of the nation are administered by HUD (the Department of Housing and Urban Development). McKinney funds originally called for grants to shelters that would provide immediate relief for the thousands of people sleeping outside, and this is precisely what occurred. Throughout the 1980s, HUD allocated funds that allowed hundreds of nonprofit corporations to open emergency shelters for the homeless. Various segments of the religious community, humanitarians, and existing nonprofits quickly made use of HUD resources, moving with great speed to provide basic shelter to get people off the streets. Functionally speaking, HUD allocations accomplished their original intention, which was to provide as many emergency beds as possible and meet the short-term needs of the homeless.

Other programs, most notably HHS (Department of Health and Human Services) funds, were to address the longer term solutions. Ninety-five percent of transitional housing program recipients and all of the permanent housing for the handicapped homeless were HUD awards to nonprofit corporations. Even religious organizations, restricted in many cases because of their evangelistic intentions, became a substantial portion of the grant recipients. Emergency funds for shelter space met the goal of providing basic food and shelters services for the homeless.

There were problems almost immediately. Budgets for most shelters are hybrids. Unlike HHS allocations which pay for staff costs, HUD funds are intended to be spent on "bricks and mortar," on items such as construction, rehabilitation, and operational costs for the structure, and not for the program. The philosophy behind this is that HUD money is intended only for shelter and housing, so the allocation is restricted to these purposes. Whatever staff is needed for the structure must be generated from other resources. In most cases, HHS funding does not complement HUD funding. The result has been that shelter staff spend as much time raising funds as operating the shelter. The more time that is spent on fund-raising activities, the less is spent on helping the homeless with anything other than the most basic services. As a result, shelters refined their abilities to house bodies, often becoming massive warehouses of human beings, but they were never given the time or the resources necessary to develop interventions that could help the homeless overcome their problems.

This process was accelerated when HUD gave larger allocations to shelters that housed more people. Desiring to help as many as possible and looking to increase their budgets, shelter directors increased their capacity in order to access the funds. The result was double-edged. On the one hand, the goal of getting as many people off the street as possible was met, often by creating massive and impersonal operations. On the other hand, many of the homeless would not buy into a "Baskin-Robbins" approach of taking a number and waiting to eat, shower, and sleep. One homeless man claimed that going to a shelter was akin to being a cow at the stockyards. The most individualistic of the homeless chose to sleep outside rather than become a faceless unit of service.

The problems with these allocations are apparent to those seeking to help the homeless. HHS funds staff positions and specific programs to help the homeless, while HUD provides the facilities for the programs to take place in. In many cases, the two agencies will not fund the same program. HHS programs operate for the homeless but often in independent settings, while shelters are strapped for staff and resources for program development.

Given the current funding mechanisms, an organization can receive support for staff or for its building and operation, but not for both. Because of this, community action agencies, for example, hire staff to teach the homeless job skills but this teaching is often done somewhere other than the shelter. At the same time, shelters, the place where an abundance of homeless people stay, seek to provide intervention services but do not have the staff necessary to provide them. To access these programs, the homeless must leave where they are to find the programs, when it would be simpler to take the programs to the people.

When the McKinney Act was authorized, it called for the establishment of the Interagency Council on the Homeless, which would bring all facets of McKinney funding under one umbrella. The Interagency Council was created to be informational in its purpose, however, perhaps intending but never actually communicating the coordination of allocations. Representatives of the council share what they are doing with their respective portions of McKinney funds, even call for a better coordination of efforts, but they have never

functioned in a way that made for complementary allocations. After a decade of effort, homeless advocates are fond of
asking if the folks in Washington ever talk to one another. The
way funds are distributed leaves the impression that they do
not.

After so many years of this uneven mechanism for allocating funds, the federal government is just beginning
to admit that such an approach has not produced the desired results. While newly-funded programs and shelters
abound, so do the homeless. The response has simply not kept
pace with the escalation of homelessness. For every new
program started, for each shelter opened, the length of the
waiting list for those wishing to receive services grows. What
has become apparent is that the federal government had good
intentions when it authorized the McKinney Act, but the
leadership necessary to weld these resources into a solution
has not materialized. The short-term response of offering
basic food and shelter made an impact, but there has been no
significant action in the development of a long-term response.

While the government has thrown money at the problem,
its aim has often been off, and its good intentions have not
produced the desired results. Homelessness has not abated
but has continued to grow and change. Just as emergency
services were beginning to address the needs of men, the
homeless population began to include women, children, and
families. Rather than continue the attack on the first segment
of the population, resources were redirected toward these
new subpopulations, producing a half-hearted, never fully
armed response to the needs of all of those on the streets.

The McKinney allocations began as a great outpouring of
concern at the federal level for the homeless. As these resources made their way down to the local level, however,
they became more of a trickle to planning bodies and
nonprofits. At each descending step, lobbyists and established programs fought for and received restricted McKinney allocations. Portions of McKinney funds could only be
awarded to certain types of agencies at the federal level. For
example, HHS funds could only be received by Department

of Human Resource agencies, the state branches of HHS. The closer funds got to the local level, the greater were the restrictions on them and the less accessible they became. No clear sense of leadership was established at the national level—save perhaps Mitch Snyder—so a vacuum surrounded the newly-declared war on homelessness. Bureaucratic administrators told more service providers not to apply for funds than assisted those who could. The first battle of the war was a whimper without real leadership. Local governments looked to the state, who looked to the federal government, who delegated the entire effort to the bureaucrats.

The Interagency Council on the Homeless did share information, often hosting conferences in large cities at expensive hotels where participants could learn about how the war was going in other places. These conferences were helpful to those who attended, but the sessions often included only those who were employed at state agencies or by local governments. Those closest to the front lines—shelter directors, soup kitchen sponsors, and case managers—worked for small organizations that could not afford to send anyone to receive the information. It always seemed ironic to first-time participants from shelters that conferences on homelessness were held in a posh hotel. This is not to say such conferences were meaningless, but they often excluded the organizations that could have benefited the most from them. Those who did enjoy them were large, established agencies that already received generous McKinney allocations.

There were exceptions of course, but what leadership emerged was most often confined to the local level. These exceptions, even the notable ones, were isolated, however, and the leadership vacuum has continued, making for no significant victories in the war against homelessness. At best, local leaders have managed the homeless problem without attacking it. Regardless of how well a problem is managed, however, until it is attacked it will remain a problem. At best, many fingers have filled numerous holes in a dam, but the homeless population continues to grow.

Until there is a true, coordinated effort to allocate the available resources and implement the programs, homelessness will never abate. A war against homelessness is the same as one fought against another country. There must be a clear sense of purpose and an appropriate chain of command. Until the federal government assumes this responsibility, resources will continue to be well intended but often misguided. The government's response to homelessness has not failed, but it has certainly not succeeded.

Bluntly put, the federal government has responded to the short-term needs of the homeless but has shied away from developing a long-term vision for the people to follow. Paraphrasing the book of Proverbs, where there is no vision, the people—and the programs—perish. Strengthening the fundamental response to homelessness and any other national problem requires a long-term orientation and a sense of shared vision. It is the government's obligation to fulfill the vision formulated in the Constitution. As Peter Senge points out in his magnificent volume *The Fifth Discipline*, "Without a vision of succeeding through product innovation, pressures to divert investment into short-term problem solving will be overwhelming."[4] The allocation of resources to meet the short-term needs of the homeless has ended up institutionalizing numerous social service programs that operate with no clear sense of where they are going. Agencies exist to help people, and they certainly do, but a nebulous vision does not solve any problems.

The required vision to combat significant social problems is built on a coordinated effort and a team approach. The McKinney Act provided resources to existing efforts, most notably to the HHS, HUD, FEMA, and the Veterans Administration, and charged them with responding to homelessness as they saw fit. To the HHS, this meant crafting a response built on mental health and substance-abuse interventions. To HUD, the response was related to housing and shelter. To FEMA, the response was to provide emergency services. The Interagency Council made certain every agency knew what the other was doing, but there was little coordination. As

McKinney resources were threatened, these agencies began to compete with one another for continued funding. Such a context does not allow for the development of a team approach.

To build a coordinated response, according to Peter Drucker, "You ask: What are we trying to do? Then, what are the activities?"[5] In its haste to offer a solution, the government funded activities but never asked exactly what they were trying to accomplish. With no clear vision and at best superficial teamwork, activities were established and continue, but little is actually being accomplished—unless the goal is only to feed and shelter the homeless. Any other expectations from the war on homelessness leave one wondering what we will be left with once all the resources are gone.

Allocations are the key to getting these agencies to work in concert. By their very nature, all organizations are turf oriented, protecting their own programs and seeking to insure their continued existence. This is true at the federal level as well as the local. Normally, forcing organizations to work together, to jointly use their resources in a collective manner, is the only way to generate a true broad-based response. The government response to homelessness was set to fail from the beginning when it did not tie allocations to program development. The McKinney Act used existing programs as they were, not calling on them to work together to distribute the funds. There was no provision to insure complementary allocations and the McKinney response was a shotgun effort at best, firing a smattering of resources at the problem. As such, pieces of the problem, but never the whole, have been addressed.

Because of this uneven approach, the government allowed the existing programs to continue serving a certain need but never established a framework that would produce wide-ranging results. Organizations can, therefore, rattle off how many meals have been served, how many nights lodging have been provided, how much medication has been dispensed, and how many jobs have been found, but no agency can claim that homelessness has been addressed in any significant way. The McKinney response has been akin to the Great Society's War on Poverty. An effective response to the new homeless would have learned from the mistakes of that 1960s effort—it would have cut out competition for resources, disallowed the development of programs that enable homelessness to continue in any form, and maintained programs because of desired results rather than longevity.

Make no mistake, there are several programs that are waging a successful war on homelessness. Public and private efforts that do produce desirable results have grown. These efforts do help the homeless overcome their condition and become productive members of society again. They should be encouraged and supported. If possible, they should be replicated. There are too many programs, however, that simply serve the want and never address the problem. These programs should be forced to change their purpose or simply be cut. The measure of effectiveness should be whether or not the effort produces the desired results—getting the homeless out of their poverty at acceptable levels. The successful efforts are typically the best run and most cost-efficient.

Rather than creating numerous programs in myriad institutions, each which exists to perpetuate itself, programs should be collapsed into common efforts that meet the needs of the homeless where they are—in the shelters or on the streets—and that see them completely through the intervention. Such a process starts by defining the desired result, then identifies the activities necessary to meet the goals, and finally asks what is the appropriate funding mechanism.

The government began at the wrong end of this cycle. First, it established how much was going to be spent. Second, it identified how this money was going to be allocated. Third, it asked what specific activities it was going to spend the money on. Fourth, it assumed that the result given was the desired one. It is little wonder that homelessness has not abated but continues to grow. Even worse, there is the fear that the mistakes of the welfare system, establishing programs that enable people to live in poverty, have been instituted all over again.

The response that government has led the nation to pursue is one that ultimately does not work. Certainly, homeless people are helped, but there is no vision to eradicate homelessness, only an effort to control and manage it. Programs that receive government support are able to treat the symptoms of homelessness, but not the causes. While agencies are encouraged to work together, there are few, if any, mechanisms in place to make certain they do. The majority of programs work independently of one another minimizing their overall effectiveness. Most importantly, the government has neglected to provide any real sense of leadership, and the ensuing vacuum has allowed for a response that includes superficial cooperation, little coordination, much competition, and the development of institutional protectionism. Never has the government led the country to address anything other than short-term goals.

Such an approach neglects the lessons learned from history. During the Great Depression of the 1930s, government responded to the housing needs of the nation with the development of public housing. The Housing Act of 1937 arose out of the dire housing needs of a large portion of the country's population. In his 1937 inaugural address, President Franklin Roosevelt estimated that one-third of the people in the United States were ill-housed. The New Deal legislation included federal initiatives to meet these housing needs. The Housing Act of 1937 sought to "remedy the unsafe and unsanitary housing conditions and the acute shortage of decent, safe, and sanitary dwellings."

This would be accomplished by doing away with slum dwellings and creating new units by granting forty-year loans to local housing authorities, which would develop and administer the projects. It is important to note the federal government's basic assumptions about the housing problem. The housing ills of the country were thought to be short-term, related to the massive unemployment being experienced. "Roosevelt himself thought of his housing programs less as a way to aid slum dwellers than as a way to revive a sick industry—nearly a third of the jobless were in the building trades," explains historian Joseph Alsop.[6] The government believed that if the job situation was addressed, the housing needs would be met. Thus the Housing Act was conceived to meet both needs at once: have the jobless build new units, thus stimulating local economies, and then move into them, thus addressing the housing needs. Such a well-intentioned but simplistic response to a massive social ill did meet the short-term goals established by the government, but as there were no long-term objectives, public housing soon became institutionalized.

All one need do is drive through any public housing project in the country to see the results of such an approach. Old structures are in dire need of rehabilitation, as the alternative to slum dwellings quickly became slums themselves. Public housing has met the needs of three generations of Americans, forcing housing authorities to become permanent landlords rather than administrators of short-term assistance. The projects are now being scaled down, with many units razed, so that they may be more efficient in the long run. When funds are not available to upgrade the projects, deteriorating units are boarded up. The target population of public housing has changed from anyone needing decent housing to those considered most desirable. The result is not what anyone imagined. While needy people are helped, the public housing institution (like many other welfare programs) has become an enabler of poverty. Seeking to address only short-term goals, the federal government created long-term problems.

There is the potential for a similar scenario with the government's response to the homeless. Shelters and other programs created to meet the needs of the homeless are only based on short-term, reactionary goals. While many individuals are being helped, the problem itself is not being addressed. When it comes to social ills, government response is almost always reactionary, rarely taking the initiative to be preventive. Being proactive is a concept the government is fond of talking about, but rarely implements itself. Until the government recognizes the desired results of an effective response to homelessness—the eradication of homelessness for all who do not choose that life style—its programs may end up enabling the problem to continue for generations to come.

Homelessness "reveals unresolved political, economic, and social questions that are often painful to face. Programs that seriously address homelessness push the resolution of important concerns of our times and are involved in controversy with others in the community almost by definition."[7] Without a clear resolve to help the homeless and a clearly defined purpose with stated outcomes, responses to the homeless inevitability lead to controversy, competition, and ultimately, failure. As the government has responded to the changing needs of a new homeless population, it has failed to exercise any true leadership. The government response can be characterized as reacting to issues as they have cropped up. As the homeless population continued to change, so did the response. As communities reacted to the government response, programs have continuously changed, never allowing for consistent interventions. Government-sponsored programs have been as transitory as the homeless themselves are often thought to be.

Without clear leadership from the top and no real emergence of grass roots leadership at the state and local level, many looked to other institutions for a sense of vision. While some argue that the government bears sole responsibility for helping the homeless, others claim that it is the church's obligation. In reality, homelessness is a social ill of such proportions that it will take both institutions working in concert to find true solutions. For many, the religious community is seen as the most logical institution to meet the needs of those living on the streets. Like the government, however, the church's response has been well-intentioned but not clear in its goals. Also like the government, the overall response of the religious community has been insufficient.

FOUR

THE RELIGIOUS RESPONSE: CHARITY, NOT COMMUNITY

In his rallying cry for the Atlanta Project, relates Gayle White of the *Atlanta Constitution*, former President Jimmy Carter "called the area's churches 'basically a dormant element of self-gratification and security'—a 'plastic shell' that protects people from the outside world."[1] When it comes to the homeless, some churches and synagogues do a great deal, while most do nothing. Yet the religious community is the one institution with a clear mandate to help the poor. As Noah Snider writes,

> *Whether we profess to be Christian, Jew, Moslem, or a follower of another faith, with rare exception, [we have been] given the mandate to help the poor and the homeless. The directive is explicit. The benefits for compliance and the consequences for not doing so are also clearly detailed. . . . The New Testament, the Torah, the Koran, all mandate certain action toward the poor. Within virtually all religious writings, we find divine instruction to those who can reach out to those who need help.[2]*

The Old and New Testaments contain numerous calls to share what one has with those who have nothing. The Levitical law demands that one allow the homeless to move into one's own home at no charge (Lev. 25:35–38). The prophet Isaiah, when describing the service required by the Lord, tells the reader to "bring the homeless poor into your home" (58:7). Throughout the Torah, there is the challenge to remember "the widow, the orphan, and the sojourner."

In the New Testament, Jesus roots his ministry in "preaching good news to the poor" (Luke 4:18). Throughout his life, he identified strongly with the poor, at one point even saying that he was homeless: "Foxes have holes, and birds of the air have nests, but the Son of Man has no place to lay his head" (Luke 9:58). The early church took in individuals without families and grafted them into a "new" family. The homeless were key members of the early church. Some of the letters of the New Testament are addressed to the paroikia, the homeless aliens in a strange land.[3] Indeed, the early church made many efforts to include the poor, the destitute, and the outsider into their fellowship. It may be said that the early church attempted to be a social network for those who had no significant relationships. For the poor, the Christian community provided a more than adequate substitution for the sort of friendly affiliation, including common meals, that a person of that time might otherwise have sought in clubs, guilds, or cultic association.[4]

The same principles are found in other major faiths. "'Eastern religions believe giving good produces virtue,' according to Dr. John Y. Fenton of Emory University. 'It produces good karma to give money away.'"[5] The Koran also stresses the importance of showing kindness to the helpless. Giving alms to the poor is thought to be one of the pillars of the Islamic faith.

With all major religions attaching such significance to caring for the poor, why have modern religious institutions shunned them? In spite of some very creative and meaningful ministries established for the homeless, most local congregations express little concern for them. Aside from the sporadic storefronts, soup kitchens, and emergency shelters that are considered to be related ministries, congregations are not engaged with the homeless. Religious institutions often cite how much they spend on benevolence as an indication of their concern for the poor. When this amount is compared to total budgets, however, it is insignificant. It is most ironic that, while the homeless need social support systems more than anything else and congregations are in the business of establishing a sense of community, the two groups have little to do with one another. The single greatest sign most congregations give to the homeless is locked doors. This is true even though church buildings are called sanctuaries. For the homeless, these buildings are often painful reminders they are not wanted, even by those who claim to care for them.

The church universal is one of the few, if not only, groups with the potential to facilitate social networks on a massive scale. The structure and the mandate to integrate the homeless and the marginal into mainstream society are already in place. The religious community simply needs to take seriously the fulfilling of one of its primary goals. Specifically, the religious community is charged with "evangelizing" those who are outside of a congregation to help them become functioning members of a socially accepted group. The "good news" is that these social networks are available to those who will take advantage of them.

To be sure, this is a different view than most religious people have of evangelism. Still, in an age when many have little use for religious institutions, such a move would be a bold, new effort to reintroduce many to the validity and usefulness of being a member of a congregation. If such an attitude toward evangelism were developed and implemented, both the homeless and the local congregation would be helped. The homeless would have social support systems, and the church would have fulfilled its mandate.

While the majority of congregations do not make outreach to the homeless a priority, there are many models from which they can learn. If congregations wish to fulfill their mission to minister "even to the least of these," they must sacrifice homogeneous fellowship in favor of diversity. Current expressions of the faithful community share very little with their first-century counterparts. What is the relationship of today's church with the homeless? Using Francis M. Dubose's classification of churches, one begins to understand some of the reasons why the majority of mainline congregations make only nominal attempts to integrate the poor into their fellowship.[6] Just because a congregation is in close proximity to a need does not necessarily mean that efforts will be made to minister to and meet that need. Since the majority of homeless people are located in urban areas (although there are increasing numbers of rural homeless), this chapter will concentrate only on urban churches.

Each metropolitan area has a downtown, or "old first," church. This church draws members from a wide radius. The facility is typically large and elaborate and near the central business district. It frequently offers social ministries. As the homeless often reside in or near this area, they are usually aware of the old first church. Aside from emergency assistance programs, however, few attempts are made to include the marginal, who live in the shadows of the building.

Many downtown churches employ elaborate security systems to keep out the undesirable. The homeless are seen only through social ministry programs as clients or objects to receive aid. Programs that are relational in nature do not actively seek to include the homeless, who often stand outside during prayer services or fellowship meals. There are exceptions, but most old first churches pay scant attention to the homeless. Many use their church social minister who regulates involvement with the homeless through emergency assistance efforts, and, through these agencies, the congregation feels it is doing its part.

On a visit to Washington, D.C., I toured an old first church and was amazed to discover an expensive security system used to keep out the "troublemakers." The senior pastor explained the historic tradition of the church as he led me around the immaculate facility. He listed the numerous projects the congregation sponsored. As I left, I witnessed a number of homeless people on the church grounds, seeking warmth in the shrubs. Living in the shadows of the old first church, they were rarely invited in. Yet the congregation felt it was doing its part through formal ministry programs. This appears to be a typical picture for many old first churches.

Neighborhood churches are scattered across metropolitan areas. Drawing primarily from local residents, these congregations are either stable or declining in membership. Often, they struggle for continued existence. Many are located near pockets of homelessness. There is usually little contact between these congregations and the homeless, however, as the congregation tries to perpetuate itself by attracting more community residents. The homeless are perceived as a symbol of the neighborhood's decline, with many churches attributing a drop in attendance to factors like the presence of "riffraff." There is rarely any organized, positive interaction.

Often, neighborhood churches will attempt ministries to reach residents, usually in the form of emergency assistance. One fellowship decided to begin a clothing closet and held a clothing drive. A room was designated and volunteers were recruited to staff the ministry. When all was ready, a sign was placed in the front door and announcements ran in the church newsletter. After a few weeks, the volunteers decided the effort was a failure. Only a handful of individuals, mostly church people, had taken advantage of the available clothing. The workers quit and the effort ceased. Members talked about how they had tried to reach out to the homeless, but their efforts were not appreciated. Congregations remember such aborted attempts whenever they are challenged to help the homeless. The majority of neighborhood churches express only superficial concern for the homeless in their communities.

Suburban churches are typically located on the city's perimeter. These congregations often have the greatest resources and emphasize mission involvement. They are normally located too far from the central city to have much interaction with the homeless, and thus they concern themselves only in indirect ways. The members support mission work and shelters for the homeless through contributions. Many host speakers who educate them about ministries with the homeless. Nevertheless, there is little organized interaction. In spite of this, many suburban congregations are a source of volunteers and charitable contributions to help meet the basic needs of the homeless. According to the *Atlanta Constitution*, "Some 35.5 percent of suburban congregations reported involvement in housing or shelter for the homeless" in Atlanta, Georgia, "and many feel it is more appealing to send money to Russia or Africa than to homeless people only twenty miles away."[7] While suburban congregations have tremendous potential, in most cases they would rather contribute money to the homeless than invite them to participate in the fellowship.

One of the few attempts to reach the homeless comes from storefront churches. These "congregations" typically rent a small area in or near the central business district where music and preaching services are held. Passersby are compelled to come in. The message is pure hellfire and damnation, the emphasis is sin, and homelessness is reduced to a moral condition. The homeless are told that if they give their lives to Jesus, things will be better. They may not be able to improve their earthly existence, they are told, but they will be rewarded in heaven. Invitations into the fellowship are long and drawn out. Conversions rarely occur and there is little growth. There is no real attempt to build relationships, as the only concern is saving souls.

On a visit to a storefront church in Louisville, Kentucky, I witnessed this type of "ministry" personally. The gospel message was preached from a loudspeaker that hung over the front door. "Come in, sinner! Turn away from your wicked ways!" Entering the small room, I took a seat in the back row and felt the preacher directing all attention to me. Once the message was concluded, the small congregation of ten or fifteen sang "Just as I Am." After singing all stanzas twice, I suspected everyone was waiting for me to do something. The preacher kept his gaze directed at me. Finally, I walked the aisle and introduced myself as a minister. Immediately the music stopped and the service concluded. The preacher asked questions about my "flock" as he led me to the door. Once outside, he promised to keep me in his prayers. Most of the congregation got in their cars and drove home to their own neighborhoods. They would return the following night.

A difference between traditional congregations and storefront congregations is their view of homelessness. Traditional congregations see homelessness as a social condition and as a moral failure. The nature of their faith dictates their response to human problems. Many attempt direct ministries, and most support "mission" efforts to respond to basic human needs. These institutions feel they should do something, but they are often at a loss for how to respond to social ills that they know little about. As a result, they contribute money and feel they are doing their part. Storefront congregations, on the other hand, simply see homelessness as a moral condition. For them, this world is evil, and the best the religious community can do is prepare for the afterlife. If the homeless will make a profession of faith, these congregations feel they have done everything they can for these "sinners." The homeless may still sleep outside, but they will be in the arms of Jesus after death.

Most consistent efforts to reach the homeless are through nonchurch initiatives. Interdenominational shelters were among the first to meet the needs of the homeless. These missions offer shelter, food, and worship opportunities. Individuals from other congregations volunteer to preach at services that resemble those of the storefront congregations. Worship is viewed as a complement to the meeting of basic needs. Thus the values of traditional congregations are merged with the "spiritual" emphasis of the storefront.

These types of efforts, best illustrated by the Salvation Army and Union Mission, try to go beyond simple charity, combining aspects of spirituality, but community is not incorporated into the approach. These efforts often draw financial support from traditional congregations and are viewed as mission projects. They are normally overwhelmed by the number of homeless people requesting services.

There are many efforts by individual congregations to respond to the needs of the homeless. Most, however, emphasize emergency food, clothing, shelter, and religious services. Few attempts are made to nurture a conversion by an indigent person. Interaction between congregations and the homeless is nominal and does not emphasize relationships. In short, congregations do things for the homeless and not with them. The religious response to homelessness is rooted in charity and while this is certainly an appropriate place to begin, congregations do not go one step further to include the homeless in the community.

The religious community does not extend the same invitation to the poor that it offers others. Congregations do not make it their business to include the homeless as members of their community. When confronted with the challenge of how to respond to the homeless, the religious community argues over just what that response should be. As Smith and Barndt put it, the very act of arguing over the question "What should be the church's response to the poor and oppressed? . . . [reveals] a belief that 'the church' is something quite separate from the 'poor and oppressed';. they are two different things responding to each other, rather than one and the same thing. When the church is not seen as rooted in and identified with the broken ones, then the poor and oppressed are clearly outsiders, and the only response . . . will of course be condescending, paternalistic charity."[8] Such a response is in obvious contradiction to the significance all major religions attach to caring for the poor. It is little wonder the religious community's current response to homelessness is token in comparison to its potential response. There is no question that the church, the synagogue, and the mosque can contribute more to the war against homelessness.

How can the religious community respond? Placing monetary concerns aside for the moment, there are numerous ways to begin. A congregation can first establish a relationship with the homeless. Because there are so many different types of homelessness, the response should be built around specific needs and not generalized ideas about who the homeless are thought to be. Too often, congregations start ministries built around perceived needs, and not what is actually needed. For example, a soup kitchen or a clothes closet makes little sense when there are other such programs within walking distance of the building. In short, the target group must be clearly identified, and then the target need must be clearly established.

The congregation must then set goals and objectives for working with the homeless. What services will be offered? How will they be carried out? Who will be responsible? What methods of evaluation will be used? How much will it cost? The entire congregation will have to become involved in the answers to these questions if the effort is to succeed.

Next, an adequate pool of volunteers must be enlisted. This is one of the strengths of the religious community. Services offered by nonprofessionals are more readily accepted by the homeless than those offered by professionals. The homeless, like anyone else, know when someone is willingly spending time with them and when someone is doing it as part of a job. They understand the difference between someone who wants to be their friend and someone who is paid for being a friend. Congregations should, by their nature, be about the business of establishing relationships with those outside the community. Further, the homeless need significant support systems to make any real progress in overcoming their poverty. If the religious community actively adheres to its call to care for the poor, and if the homeless respond to these acts of friendship, both will be better off as a result. The homeless will cease being faceless statistics, and the congregation will grow in number and fulfill its calling.

As inroads are established with individual street people, volunteers will be called upon to assist in an vast array of "personal" problems. Homelessness will cease being a social ill too big to handle and will become a series of hurdles that must be overcome. The homeless often need help in navigating the maze of bureaucratic red tape required to obtain birth certificates, identification cards, benefits, and health care. They need a network of reliable friends if they are to find day care, job tips, transportation to and from work, and safe and affordable housing. Members of the congregation usually have the resources necessary to help the homeless address these needs.

Of course, not all homeless people will meet the expectations of congregations to become self-sustaining, productive members of society. Some are simply not capable of complete independence. The mentally ill, the substance abusers, the poorly educated, those released from prison— all need bridges built to help them back to self-sufficiency. These people need extra care and compassion. They will tax the patience of anyone, even those who are religiously motivated to help them. Still, the religious community is the one group that exists to address the physical, social, emotional, and spiritual needs of people. The congregation must struggle to be always open to new ways in which to minister, even if it means becoming primary supporters for those who have gone as far as they can down the road to self-sufficiency.

Religious institutions must begin the process of making themselves available to the homeless in ways they most need. First and foremost, the concept of sanctuary must be reclaimed. Too many religious buildings function more like private clubs for members only rather than sanctuaries. A sanctuary is a place of refuge for those in turmoil. The vast majority of religious buildings in this country convey the opposite message. Sadly, religious institutions reflect "the

American tendency to value property over life" says David Claerbaut in *Urban Ministry*.[9] Until this attitude changes, religious buildings will continue to resemble office buildings more than living sanctuaries.

Congregations must begin to make their buildings available to those who need them the most. Religious buildings often sit empty most of the week. This is poor stewardship when, with relative ease, the buildings could function as "cool centers" during the heat of summer and "warm stations" in the harsh winter season. Pews make excellent overnight beds for emergency shelters. Baptismal pools make great bathtubs for those in need of hygienic care. Sunday school rooms may be converted into apartments. Areas for storage might be offered to men and women who have no place to keep their belongings. Phones may be made available to those who need them. The principle of people being more important than buildings must be central if the religious community is going to include the needy. Buildings are little more than tools used to carry out ministries.

Such a perception is contrary to the way most congregations view their facilities. Functioning more like museums than sanctuaries, religious buildings have become more akin to the empty tomb that Jesus left behind than places of life-filled fellowship. When congregations focus on people rather than structures, this perception has a way of correcting itself. One congregation in Atlanta, Georgia, decided to make itself available to the homeless. Volunteers set up mats on the floor, prepared hot drinks and a simple meal, and offered other services to the homeless. After a short time, the congregation began to rethink why it was doing these things. "Church members adjusted to the few stains that appeared on the sanctuary carpet; they were part of the price of what they had undertaken, examining old values, images and expectations," explains Mary Ellen Hombs and Mitch Snyder in *Homelessness In America*.[10]

Inevitably, however, the question of money arises. The congregation will want to know how much it will cost them to care. For many religious institutions it is merely a question of where they wish to place their emphasis—on buildings or on helping people. Congregations that have a difficult time maintaining their ministries will not be able to afford to spend money to help the homeless. There are still many things they can do, however. Many of the ideas already cited can be easily implemented by congregations with tight budgets. Any congregation can include the homeless in their community, and every church, synagogue, or mosque should become a referral agent for the homeless. There are a host of service agencies located near every congregation in America. Congregations who cannot, or will not, engage in more costly ministries can tell the homeless where they can receive help. A directory of services can be shared with anyone who asks for help. At the very least, congregations should know where to send the homeless for help if they cannot, or will not, provide it.

What prevents the religious community from doing these things? In most cases it is the clergy. According to Dieter Hessel, "Pastoral literature typically views social ministries as elective activities for specialized persons and ecumenical agencies, or as a subcategory of community relations. Pastors and church officers generally are cautioned to avoid overinvolvement in social concerns, lest preaching, teaching, caring, celebrating, fund-raising, and administration may be slighted!"[11] Because of the role government has taken in addressing the social needs of the country, ministers have become willing to concentrate on "spiritual" matters, leaving temporal concerns to others. Forsaking scriptural mandates to care for the poor, churches cite the separation of church and state as the principal foundation for religious activity. According to E. Glenn Hinson, religious organizations, which have "so much to gain by the separation of church from state, etched this outlook deeply into their consciousness. The result is that they have allowed themselves to tiptoe into social concern only with the most extreme caution."[12] Social activism has, therefore, been divided into safe and not so safe—even dangerous—

categories. Examples of safe social action are abortion (for or against), separation of church and state, children's issues, pornography, and nationalism. Each of the stances congregations take on these issues are rooted in Scripture and religious tradition.

The antiabortion activities carried out by many religious communities, for example, are rooted in scriptural principles. God is the author of life. As such, God, and therefore a follower of God, cannot be a destroyer of life. Some congregations have become so strongly convinced of the truth of their stance, that they step out on faith, replicate many of the methods used by 1960s antiwar protestors, and dive wholeheartedly into social action. Rather than being the rule, however, such activity is the exception. It is interesting to note how religious communities carefully pick and choose which social activities they will become engaged in. While scriptural mandates cover everything from feeding the hungry to improving race relations, the religious community seems to have delegated many responses to government and social service agencies. Only on those issues of an appropriate "spiritual" caliber—normally those that do not call for much personal sacrifice—are members encouraged to become actively engaged. Such tiptoeing has become the norm for the religious community.

In the 1980s, evangelist Billy Graham entered the discussion of the church's role in solving social problems. Grounded in the revivalist tradition, for years Graham had exemplified missionary zeal. From his support of Joseph McCarthy to his unfailing loyalty to Richard Nixon, Graham was well known for his leanings to the political right. Many felt that Graham best represented typical religious beliefs in America. Drawing from Graham's example and the work of other evangelicals, Kenneth Leech concludes, "The history of American revivalism provides a depressing picture in terms of social outlook."[13] The majority of religious institutions simply have not concerned themselves with social issues. As Hinson says of the beliefs of many in the Christian church: "The business of the churches is to be spiritual, to save souls. The church should not become involved in matters that belong to the province of the state."[14] This is not to say that religious institutions have not been involved in social *services*. They have. But most churches have drawn the line at social *action*.

One can easily imagine, then, the surprise of many when Graham began to speak out against the nuclear arms race and war. Defying the wishes of President Reagan, he conducted a preaching crusade in the then Soviet Union. This action was a clear joining of the spiritual world with the political. Protesting the nuclear arms race had already become an acceptable cause with much of the religious world, but Graham's stance was still controversial for someone of his stature. While his stance was a token expression of social action—the position statements written by the U.S. Catholic Bishops are more notable examples of spiritual motivation in the political world—the shock that Graham's actions caused demonstrates that mainstream American religious institutions do not support social action. So long as this kind of social action is the exception rather than the rule, the influence of the religious community will be largely insignificant in addressing the social concerns of the country.

Most religious institutions clearly view issues such as homelessness as unsafe if they are addressed at anything other than a superficial level. Homelessness without social action—without taking political stances—is simple charity. The majority of the religious community's interaction with the homeless is in helping to address the most basic of needs. Targeting homelessness for social action demands a higher level of commitment and a redirection of institutional resources. Including the homeless in a congregation—indeed, doing anything more than meeting the most basic of needs—would force the congregation to think about policy issues. This would also force the entire religious community to examine its faith in light of public policy. By and large, religious leaders are not willing to do this.

The lack of inclusion of diverse people stems from a

second reason the religious community does not choose to respond to homelessness at anything other than a superficial level. Congregations have become homogeneous in their composition. Members are all from more or less the same economic background, have similar educations, dress the same, talk the same, and look the same. As Larry McSwain contends, "In the past, . . . neighborhoods have formed along social class, racial, and ethnic uniformity. So the [religious institution] developed as a reflection of its neighborhood homogeneity."[15] As such, ministries developed by the congregation typically reflect the needs of that particular group of people. Ministries and programs that are geared toward another social group are viewed as radical in nature, going above and beyond the expectations of the church, synagogue, or mosque. Such programs allow the congregation to believe it is fulfilling its scriptural mandates by doing things *for* the homeless, not *with* them. When religious institutions opt for charity rather than community, their "help" functions as an enabler of homelessness and perpetuates a homogeneous congregation. "The task of the gospel," concludes McSwain, "is not to call persons to a white Anglo-Saxon Protestantism. It is not to call persons to a black cultural experience, nor to a Mexican or Brazilian cultural experience. [Religious expressions should be] . . . transcultural."[16] While the vast majority of American religious institutions call for inclusion, they rarely practice it.

If organized religion is going to make a significant difference for the homeless, it must become an inclusive community. Congregations must actively recruit people who are different. They must cultivate a respect for "being different." Dolores Leckey suggests that "differentiation and 'being different' is . . . the realization that God and grace are not reserved for conformity."[17] Throughout the development of American religious institutions, congregations have become increasingly exclusive of some segments of society. As congregations became more homogeneous, they shut their doors to groups such as the homeless. Instead of washing their hands completely of the homeless, they have developed "mission" projects to meet the needs of the excluded groups. Separate, but not so equal, treatment has been given to those outside of the fellowship.

Until congregations fully recover the appropriate emphasis on community homelessness will continue and, to use the words of Jesus, the poor will always be with us. What should congregations do? Assuming that they accept the mandates to care for the poor and that they wish to include the poor in their expressions of faith, first they must see the homeless primarily as people—not as social problems. Often, when *individuals* are encountered, congregations respond accordingly.

Second, according to Michael Roschke, the congregation must help the person with "whatever his or her felt need is, holistically."[18] If he is hungry, the congregation gets him food. If she needs a job, they help her find work. If he needs child care before looking for a job, they provide him with child care. The congregation assumes responsibility for enabling the homeless individual to "have wholeness." Further, the congregation allows "a relationship to develop between the helper and the helpee, and to let those tags dissipate, so that people are beginning to reciprocate in ministry to one another."[19] Often, this is a time-consuming process, but the congregation must seek to make a long-term, not a short-term difference.

The third step, Roschke says, is to get the person who came for help "involved in a . . . caring community." The goal is not to convert the person to the faith, although that will certainly be a primary motivation for many, but to enter into community. When the homeless enter the congregation, both groups should be helped as a result. The homeless are introduced to the support system needed to overcome poverty, and the community grows. As this relationship continues, the homeless begin to rely less on the congregation for tangible support and are able to contribute in return.

Were the religious community in America to take such an

approach in responding to the homeless, it would certainly be slow going. Even if each congregation in the country entered into one relationship with someone experiencing homelessness, the problem would not be solved overnight. The short-term results would likely be very insignificant. The long-term results, however, would be very positive, with the congregation providing an ongoing support mechanism to insure that the person doesn't repeat homelessness. It would mean hard work. It is often difficult to be the initiator of relationships; sustaining them can be even tougher. The religious community is the only institution given such a charge. While it may not have embraced this charge wholeheartedly, it has not completely denied it, either. There is still the possibility that the religious community will live up to its convictions. If it does so, the words of the Talmud will ring true: the world will have been saved one neighbor at a time.

FIVE

THE LOCAL RESPONSE: FRAGMENTED COORDINATION

When homelessness began to be noticed by the public as a local problem, overnight shelters and emergency soup kitchens opened their doors as a response to what was thought to be a temporary crisis. Existing organizations were adapted or new ones were created to cope with the crisis. "Leaders of local sheltering efforts" according to the New York Department of Social Services, "attained the role of coordinator based upon their immediate availability, willingness to donate time and energy, and capacity to exercise leadership in a crisis atmosphere. Basically, a willingness to do the work determined who administered most new shelters."[1] Clergy, government employees, elected officials, and private citizens committed themselves to developing a response to those experiencing the most visible form of poverty the community had ever known.

There has always been homelessness, and there has always been some response in place. In the 1980s, when the problem became visible at a local level, the Salvation Army and Union Mission shelters were already established in many cities. These organizations catered to the needs of transients, alcoholics, and hobos who, for whatever reason, chose a homeless life-style. When the homeless population began to include people who did not choose homelessness, these institutions did not alter their programs to meet changing needs. As a result, the religious community, with resources made available by local municipalities, began to operate new programs geared toward the basic needs of the new homeless. Many congregations founded soup kitchens to ensure basic nutrition. Recognizing that a full stomach did not prevent people from sleeping on subway grates or in abandoned buildings, the religious community also began opening shelters to house the new homeless. The development of shelters has been the local community's primary response to the growing homeless population.

Two basic types of shelters emerged in the 1980s. First, the classic "soup and salvation" shelter assumes that meeting basic needs of food and shelter is its principal purpose. Food is served until it runs out and lodging is provided to as many as space allows. The guiding motivation of these shelters is meeting the requirements of Scripture. Normally, only food and basic lodging are provided. Staff is minimal, and there is a heavy dependence on volunteers from supporting congregations. Few records are kept, and little, if any, thought is given to why people are homeless. The only intake procedure is a quick frisking, and there are normally only two rules: no violence and no drinking. The operating policy is to allow anyone to use the shelter and to avoid forcing the homeless to do anything they do not choose to do. The rudimentary services provided are basic referral, with the primary concern being safety and crisis management. There are rarely additional programs to help the homeless, as these would be beyond the purview of the shelter's purpose.

The second type of shelter to emerge was more structured. In the mode of the Salvation Army, these shelters allow for longer residency and place emphasis on shelter rules. Individuals may remain so long as they do not violate established rules and regulations. Food, shelter, clothing, substance-abuse intervention, and worship services are the basic programs offered. Primary services are delivered by the staff, with volunteers used to augment their efforts. There is also emphasis on placing the homeless in a highly structured setting under much supervision, which helps to identify personal problems and possible solutions. Programs are established to meet the most common problems faced by homeless people. These include drug- and alcohol-abuse treatment, job training, housing searches, and worship services. The purpose of these shelters is to enable the homeless to overcome their poverty.

The homeless are encouraged to work at these shelters, performing basic chores such as cleaning, cooking, sorting through donations, and, ultimately, serving as shelter supervisors. In many cases, compensation involves a small stipend, room and board, and a few extra perks for full-time jobs. Such arrangements allow shelters to maintain low operating budgets and still have the "staff" necessary to function in an appropriate fashion. Rooted in a "pull yourself up by your own bootstraps" philosophy, such programs do assist many to overcome their homelessness. The shelter offers work to a constant pool of "employees" who can take advantage of the opportunity made available to them. Those who do not perform well are terminated, often barred from the shelter, and must look for opportunities to help themselves elsewhere.

As the local religious community mobilized to meet the basic emergency needs of the homeless, local governments struggled to get a handle on the problem. Community business leaders and private citizens called on elected officials to do something about the people living on the streets. Special task forces and blue-ribbon committees were appointed to determine whether the homeless were worthy of a community commitment to planning, funding, and providing services and to establish some "hard facts" on the nature of local homeless populations. Even though service providers knew some of the facts based on their experience with the homeless, public servants and community leaders wanted documented information about the composition and needs of the homeless population, information that could guide increased involvement.

Not only was documentation lacking, but there was misinformation about who the homeless were. The most commonly held public perception was that the homeless were from somewhere else, were all mentally ill, and were in the community only to access public benefits. Most of these myths were negative, stereotypical generalizations that were expressed by individuals who did not want "those kind of people" around their neighborhoods or businesses. These individuals did not believe that the community should expand or upgrade services to the homeless, fearing that such actions would attract more homeless people to the area. At the same time, service providers faced increasing demands for shelters, beds, food, and other forms of emergency assistance. Community leaders trying to find long-term solutions were concerned about the validity of short-term approaches and the increasing requests for funding from the emerging shelter programs.

Numerous groups sprang up seeking to bridge the gap between service providers and local governments. Task forces on vagrancy, shelter advocates, coalitions for the homeless, long-range planning committees, housing coalitions, and other such groups all developed programs that would provide the community with a course of action. Despite these numerous efforts and with little agreement on a community-wide approach, these independent actions appeared fragmented, duplicated, and often competitive. Resentments and ongoing conflicts on many sides often resulted in turf battles, misunderstanding, and continued confusion on how the community should proceed. Generally, there were high levels of distrust among the various groups and individuals involved in solving the local homeless problems. "Many district agencies with a local government," writes Catherine Zudak, "often serve the same homeless population without communicating or working together. There is little communication between city and county government. Private and nonprofit groups provide the bulk of homeless services without any input from the local government, though it may be paying for the services. This disjointed approach fails to address the complex causes and different service needs."[2] In most cases, local responses to homelessness have still not addressed such fragmentation.

These problems allowed certain individuals, agencies, and organizations to ascend to the position of overall leadership in the community. In virtually every case, however, these leaders were not elected officials or citizens of such prominence that they were able to garner a broad base of support for a cooperative system. Often, they were the same individuals who had shown the willingness to develop new programs. As they attempted to capitalize on their initial efforts and move beyond the meeting of basic food and shelter needs, they ran into opposition. As programs were devised to effectively manage homelessness at the local level, they were often overridden by the local units of government due to a fear of public outcry against increased involvement. While the community at large expressed sympathy, neighborhoods and businesses were adamant that shelters and services should be located somewhere else. Dealing with the NIMBY syndrome became the local government's principal area of interaction with the emerging local leadership. Such leadership ensured that local governments were in a reactive rather than a proactive position when dealing with homelessness.

Local governments did attempt to direct funding sources toward their community's efforts. Community development block grants, emergency shelter funds, FEMA allocations, and other resources were suddenly available from state and federal governments, and these were distributed to many of the programs devised by those who worked with the homeless. These allocations allowed for the development of additional services to assist the homeless. Job-training programs, literacy programs, and health care and mental health services were made available to service providers, leading to the creation of a new, third form of shelter.

Multipurpose shelters sought to collapse many of these services into a common program built upon the premise that it is easier to take the program to the people than to ask the people to go to a program. This premise is especially applicable to homeless people. According to Millard and Linda Fuller of Habitat for Humanity, "Surveys show that most homeless people face multiple obstacles: they may be poorly educated, drink too much, take drugs, have been in prison. They need a bridge to self-sufficiency. One of these bridges is 'transitional' housing: small super-shelters where a homeless person is helped to draw breath for a few months before moving on to a permanent home."[3] As new resources to help the homeless were made available, those providers with the longest track records added layers of programs on top of basic food and shelter services. The result of these new efforts was that, for the first time, a significant number of homeless individuals exited the shelter system, secured new housing, and reentered society as "productive" members. While these individuals were a small minority of the total number of homeless people, shelters began to talk of numerous success stories. By focusing their energies on specific subpopulations, the super-shelters could refine programs to meet particular needs. This led to the various homeless types seeking out different shelters. The chronically homeless were drawn to the no-questions-asked policy of the soup and salvation shelters. Transients and alcoholics were drawn to Salvation Army and Union Mission shelters. Those experiencing homelessness for the first time went to the super-shelters.

Each shelter type seeks to produce a different result. Soup and salvation shelters only exist to meet basic food and shelter needs. Transient shelters use basic services to expose the homeless to specific interventions. Super-shelters seek to assist individuals in overcoming the problems that made them homeless. Taken as a whole, the shelter system does *respond* to the needs of the homeless; however, it does not adequately *address* these needs. In most cases, the problem is simply managed.

Another condition contributing to this situation is that shelters do not typically communicate with one another. It is difficult to focus on larger issues and interagency coordination when personnel are overworked, understaffed, and always in crisis mode. Staff members spend the majority of their time developing the resources necessary to continue offering as many services as possible. Demand always outpaces supply. There is simply no time to consider possible linkages between other programs and the networking of various resources. No one encourages shelters to work together. Unless staff members resolve to rise above their normal routine in order to network, learn from others, and develop a common effort, they will always react to the problem they are charged to solve. Because a certain number of homeless individuals overcome their problems, staff members view these individuals as success stories and use them to justify their particular approach, with little regard to how any other agency works. Everyone may acknowledge that there is a better way to help the homeless, but most are comfortable with their routine and will not invest in change.

Shelter personnel often feel it is their job to help as many people as possible and leave the bigger questions of public policy and networking to others. Beginning with a genuine desire to help the less fortunate, they are content so long as they feel they are helping. It is not that they refuse to engage in interagency coordination. Most will if they are asked. Most of the time, however, they are not asked. They are left to focus on homelessness as they experience it, which is only within the context of their own programs. On the rare occasions when shelter operators do converse, most seek affirmation of their own approach, not viewing these conversations as opportunities to learn. The day-to-day life of never-ending crisis management in the shelter does not allow time for reflective evaluation. Shelter personnel seek affirmation of the job they are doing whenever they can get it, even if it is the sympathy of someone facing the same burdens.

The extremely high turnover rate of shelter staff further compounds the problem. The staff changes so often that there is little opportunity for relationships to develop. The stress of helping so many with so few resources leaves most feeling they are attempting to empty the ocean with a bucket. When this feeling of futility becomes prominent, they quit. Some are able to direct their energies to the development of their own routines, refining it and making it the best possible, but these employees are ultimately left with the feeling that, while they have the best possible bucket, they are still attempting to empty the ocean. They also may burn out and quit. A minority are able to stick it out, but only with grim determination.

Frederick Buechner describes how these people function when he recalls a mission where he once worked:

> It was compassion without sentimentality as much as anything else, I think—a lucid, cool, grave compassion. If it has a color, it would be a pale, northern blue. They never seem to romanticize the junkies and winos and deadbeats and losers they worked among, and they never seemed to let pity or empathy distort the clarity with which they saw them for no more if no less than what they were. . . . There was a kind of gaiety about the way they went about their work. The sadness stemmed, I suppose, from the hopelessness of their task—the problems were so vast, their resources so meager—and the gaiety from a hope beyond hope that, in the long run if not the short, all would in some holy and unimaginable way be well.[4]

This determination is fueled by the ability to remain almost exclusively focused on the help given to individuals without becoming overwhelmed by the policies and practices that create homelessness. Until shelter personnel make it their business to link with other programs, creating a network of services stronger than single efforts, they will always be enablers of the problem.

Many state agencies sponsor programs that are also part of the problem. As state agencies developed responses to homelessness, their efforts were often conceived and implemented independently of the existing shelter system. Therefore, homeless programs funded by the Department of Human Resources are often not coordinated with the shelters and other established efforts. Conceived as a way of augmenting and complementing the basic services offered by the shelters, Department of Human Resources programs developed around case management, health care, employment, and mental health services. Many of these programs work within the shelter system, delivering these services in conjunction with the shelter services.

Because these programs receive their funding from the state and do not face the almost daily fiscal crisis experienced by the shelters, they are the most stable of homeless services. There is little attention given to ensuring that the programs work in concert. It is assumed that coordination occurs at the local level, but this is rarely the case. While the original intention was to provide services that shelters were not capable of offering, local agencies often established programs that competed for the same population. When homeless organizations do work together—although many choose to function completely independent of others—it is normally through participation in a local task force or coalition.

Local task forces and coalitions for the homeless typically concentrate on policy issues and information sharing more than devising methods to coordinate efforts. Because these groups often engage in political advocacy, local units of government and other planning and funding sources do not always participate. By and large, these coalitions are comprised of service providers and a few private citizens. The primary function of these groups is to provide support for the participants. Funding issues, specific contextual problems and the desire for increased services are the regular topics of conversation. These groups are generally more active when they are reacting to events occurring in the community. Local coalitions are often the only avenue participants have to discuss their problems, and this becomes the basic purpose of many of them.

Some coalitions concentrate their activity on larger issues. These are the groups that attempt to develop needs assessments, program resources, and service information. They attempt to educate the community about the seriousness of homelessness. Initial efforts center on determining just how many are homeless in the area. These figures are anything from a guess agreed upon by the coalition to documented numbers of people served. Demographic information is then presented to the community in an effort to explain who the homeless are. Based on this information, program plans are often conceived as the group explores how to best proceed. Because these plans are developed primarily by the service providers, without the input of all segments of the community or the help of professional planners employed by local governments, they are not perceived as credible by all funding sources. The plans are thus largely ignored. While some funding sources may agree on the course of action outlined by the coalition, it takes the commitment of all funding sources in the allocation process to facilitate true coordination at the local level. The funding sources are often excluded from the planning process.

Many service providers blame the lack of coordination on chronic underfunding. Agencies compete with one another for all available resources as they become available. Because units of government do not allocate funds based on a strategy to solve the homeless problem, they slice the pie thinly to all who ask for a piece, not wanting to offend any. The result is that many homeless services have just enough financial support to continue their operations, perhaps slightly modifying them, but not enough personnel to work on comprehensive strategies. Most allocations are open to all agencies, and competition for funds is intense. Obviously, it is difficult to concentrate on coordination when agencies are fighting with one another for funding. Some feel that underfunding is an intentional strategy used by government leaders to prevent homeless advocates from working together. While local governments are often as strapped for resources as homeless advocates are, such feelings are indicative of the lack of trust among those charged with solving community problems. Until units of government together work to invest the time and resources necessary to develop a comprehensive approach to homelessness, the fragmentation of effort will continue.

Making this even more frustrating is the knowledge that if many of the existing programs were coordinated in an appropriate fashion, communities would be able to make a significant dent in the homeless problem. Governments already employ the planners needed to develop a comprehensive strategy. Various funding sources already allocate hundreds of thousands of dollars to homeless programs. Agencies already employ dedicated and knowledgeable staff members who are aware of what is needed. Churches and civic groups already provide in-kind contributions and thousands of volunteers willing to personally engage the homeless. The strengths of these resources are often negated by the fragmented coordination that occurs when no overall leader emerges to ensure maximum implementation.

Community planning organizations such as chambers of commerce and neighborhood associations—which are appropriate mechanisms for conceiving and implementing coordinated efforts—often view the homeless problem as outside their realm. Homelessness is seen as a problem that has a negative impact on tourism and the health of the community. When these organizations do involve themselves, it is often to point out that the problem is out of hand. When the community is invited to plan how to best present itself, those who work closely with social problems are excluded. The only planning that occurs is how the group will position itself *against* the problem. Many of the most effective and resourceful community leaders participate in these efforts, taking a myopic view of the community's social ills. Were the chamber of commerce to issue a call for true, broad-based, collaborative planning and then invite all interested to participate, communities would be better able to use the resources already available.

It is ironic that most segments of every community desire the same thing. Chambers of commerce do not want the homeless problem to tarnish the city's image. Religious institutions want to be inclusive. Local governments desire their citizens to live safe and fulfilled lives. Funding sources contribute money to solve the homeless problem. Citizens do not wish to see people suffering in their town. Service providers are committed to helping people. The vast majority of the homeless themselves do not want to remain on the streets. Without a catalyst to focus these energies toward the same goal, however, community resources remain underutilized as the problem worsens.

The evolution of a community response to homelessness is still in its infancy. Across the country there are examples of local governments that took the lead in forging a response. Chambers of commerce convened representatives from across the community to find an appropriate response. Local coalitions have developed working plans to better use their resources in addressing the homeless problem. Service providers in certain areas have cultivated working relationships that complement one another. Each of these efforts have had varying degrees of success and failure. In no case, however, can anyone claim to have involved everyone needed to effectively respond to homelessness. Leadership vacuums exist in all areas no matter how successful they may have been. Resources are still not used to their maximum potential. Too many people are still homeless. In spite of everything that has been done to date, it is not enough.

It is always easier to blame rather than to act. This is certainly the case with the homeless. Conservatives blame liberals for taking away the incentive to work from the poor, thus leading to homelessness. Liberals counter by

blaming conservatives for not allocating the funds necessary to meet the full range of needs. City governments
blame county governments and vice versa. Service providers blame funding sources for not allowing them to proceed full-steam ahead. Some say the church is not doing
enough, while others call for the private sector to solve the
problem. The blaming seems endless. While many call for
an end to duplicated services, no one seems willing to take
the leadership role needed to end the fragmentation of services. No one is working to pull all segments of the community together to forge a community-wide response. Politicians are fond of calling for this effort, but they rarely do
anything to make it happen.

Noah Snider argues that the effort needed to end homelessness must be similar to that mobilized for the Gulf War:
"If it were possible to gather 90 percent of our population to
support the war effort, and gather an army of several million who volunteered to die for it, is it not possible to gather
a majority who will support the repair of our society and an
army of several million who would work for it?"[5] While
many will point out that the War on Poverty failed, the idea
is a sound one. For any effort to be successful, it requires
leadership, committed resources, a common plan of action,
and the commitment to do whatever is necessary to succeed. To succeed at the local level, the community must
learn to cooperate. In most communities struggling to forge
a response to homelessness, participants have only learned
how to tolerate each other.

The greatest stumbling block to overcoming this fragmented coordination at the local level is an unwillingness
to compromise. Whenever meetings are held to discuss
what should be done about the homeless, most participants
become advocates for their own ideas first; the homeless
become secondary. Business owners will not entertain ideas
that locate a shelter near them. Landlords refuse to consider
decreasing their rents below market rates. Community
leaders do not want to discuss ways in which the homeless
may remain in the area. Service providers refuse to recog-

nize that it may be best to locate a program somewhere else. According to Gregory Pierce, "Cooperation . . . is possible only if they are willing to compromise; and politics, the art of cooperation, of group action, is at bottom nothing but the practical application of the method of cooperation."[6] It is obviously in everyone's best interest to deal with the homeless problem—but this means leaving one's baggage at the door when the opportunity for dialogue presents itself.

To cooperate, people must learn to communicate. This means listening first. Too many service providers feel that they know the answers because of their long track records. In meetings, they never tire of telling movers and shakers what must be done. Community leaders, both public and private, often view those who work with the homeless as idealistic do-gooders who have little understanding of how the world works. The more the service provider talks, the more the leaders are convinced that they are right. In meetings where there is no communication, participants leave feeling frustrated and more certain than ever that their own ideas are the only ones that matter. The meeting is viewed as meaningless. No one likes to attend such sessions. Problems are not necessarily confronted just because people sit at a common table. "Communication creates meaning for people," Warren Bennis and Burt Nanus write. "It's the only way any group, small or large, can become aligned behind . . . over-arching goals. . . . Getting the message across unequivocally at every level is the key. Basically it is what the creative process is all about."[7] Because homelessness is a relatively new social problem for communities, the burden is on those who work with the homeless to legitimize the issue for community leaders. For the most part, this has not been an agenda item for homeless advocates.

Despite the trail blazed by Mitch Snyder in calling attention to homelessness, those who work with the homeless must grow with the emerging public recognition of the problem. Many working with the homeless dress like the stereotypical homeless person, wearing faded jeans and torn shirts with antiwar slogans on them. It is hard for many community leaders to take such people seriously. More than the outward appearance, however, is the attitude projected. Advocates make demands of community leaders often without pausing to consider how their demands will be heard. Having rarely considered the larger issues, those who work directly with the homeless often reinforce the stereotype of idealistic do-gooder when making their presentations to community leaders. It is little wonder that the homeless, and those who work directly with them, are so misunderstood. Service providers have not done a good job of speaking in the idiom of the other when given the opportunity; as a result, their cause has come across as shallow, superficial, and adversarial. To best help the homeless, service providers must be accepted as such, not only by the homeless but by those who have the power and influence to mobilize the resources they so desperately need.

Those who work with the homeless must see themselves as interpreters for those who do not understand. They are always in a position to educate those around them. The way they dress, speak, and communicate influences the way they represent the homeless to those in positions to help them. Each and every meeting should be viewed as an opportunity to represent the homeless. Too often, advocates are perceived as an unprofessional bunch who are incapable of addressing complex social issues. Advocates know that feeding the hungry is more important than whether or not one wears a tie, and that providing lodging for children is of more significance than crisp creases in one's skirt. Yet those who have the ability to help often attach a great deal of significance to outward appearances. The best advocates understand this and take homelessness off the streets and into the offices where important decisions are made. Too many advocates feel that theirs is a nobler profession than is found in the private sector, and thus they have a chip on their shoulder. If the homeless are going to be represented in the way they deserve, however, advocates must pay attention to details that allow the possibility of being heard. Advocates are seen before they are heard, and first impressions are most important. This is especially true when trying to convey that the homeless are not all winos, addicts, and losers.

The way those who work with the homeless present their vocation must also reflect utmost professionalism. Too many shelters do in fact look like the stereotypical shelter. Donated clothing is piled in a corner, the walls are in need of paint, and the floor is dirty. While cleanliness may indeed be next to godliness—and next to impossible—it is fully expected by community leaders. Homeless programs are expected to be lean, efficient operations. Accountability to contributors is a necessity. Programs must be perceived as quality interventions and not as constant crisis management. All exchanges with the community deserve courtesy. Formal presentations should not be off the cuff, but carefully planned and of high quality. Flyers and other printed materials must be distributed in a businesslike manner. Larger operations should project a higher degree of professionalism. Helping the homeless is the business of caring and providers must remember that the program is a business, albeit a nonprofit one. As Peter Drucker writes, "What attracts people to an organization are high standards, because high standards create self-respect and pride."[8] Work with the homeless should not be portrayed as charity. Obviously, the organization may fall under the definition of a charitable institution, relying on the donations of others, but the daily activities must be undertaken professionally. Programs must have clear-cut goals that easily convey their purpose.

Shelters should recognize that to effectively respond to the needs of the homeless, they must have a better understanding of the problem. Too often, organizations only respond to human need when it is encountered. Homelessness is too complex for such attitudes. Shelters are laboratories in which causes of complex social issues may be studied. Statistical data should be collected throughout the year, analyzed by the staff, and reported to the community. Such presentations establish credibility in the community. While programs may meet basic needs, the causes of homelessness will not be attacked until advocates and service providers do the homework necessary to represent their cause in the best possible light.

Local responses to the homeless are first determined by those who choose to represent their cause. While many become involved simply to offer help to those in need, the job demands more than merely distributing food, clothing, and lodging. Research, networking, strategy development, coordination, compromise, follow-up, documentation, and persistence become the tools for those wishing to mobilize the entire community to respond to the problem. The community will do nothing, however, until those working with the homeless issue the call in the appropriate ways. The days of the Mitch Snyder approach are over. All informed Americans are painfully aware that homelessness exists. It is time to determine how each community should respond to its homeless population. This will only happen when those who work with the homeless recognize that it is their job to educate the community about what must be done.

NAMING THE DEMONS: SUGGESTIONS FOR A NEW RESPONSE

If the road to hell is paved with good intentions, then it is also lined with homeless people. The government, religious institutions, and local groups have forged responses to what P. J. O'Rourke calls "one of the few undeniable (and telegenic!) social injustices left." Many recognize homelessness as a problem that should not exist in the United States and have tried to do something about it. "No matter what somebody has done to himself or others," O'Rourke continues, "he doesn't deserve to freeze in the gutter."[1] For the most part, however, the response has been fragmented, idealistic, shortsighted, and shallow, signifying a lack of understanding as to why homelessness continues to grow. O'Rourke concludes that the facts are simple but misunderstood:

A government house-building orgy won't work because one-third of the homeless are screwed up on drink and drugs and will sell the plumbing. The rest have primarily economic problems, but we can't keep giving them free housing forever, and it won't help.

The law of supply and demand tells us that when the price of something is artificially set below the market level there will soon be none of that thing left—as you may have noticed the last time you tried to buy something for nothing.[2]

What will help the homeless? Are there valid suggestions to enable them to leave the streets of our cities? There are some things that can be done to begin eradicating homelessness. The first involves meeting the homeless where they are—outside.

When people are physically ill, they check into a hospital where all the services they may need in order to get better are available. In this setting, they receive an initial diagnosis that is tested on the spot to identify all contributing symptoms to the illness. Once identified, a prognosis is given, a plan of action is outlined, and the symptoms are treated with medications and interventions. Supervision is provided around the clock by orderlies, nurses, and physicians. Often, new causes of the illness are uncovered in the midst of treatment, and through a trial-and-error approach, doctors are able to develop the appropriate treatment. Usually, the patients leave the hospital well, or well enough, to resume a healthy life. If this is the acceptable course of intervention for physical ills, does it make sense to apply such an approach to social ills?

The majority of shelters and soup kitchens provide only the most basic of services—food, sleeping space, showers, and a few other niceties. These services do little to combat the problem and actually help enable the homeless to continue in their life style by offering just enough sustenance and hope to endure another day. Services become ends unto themselves, with success measured in terms of how many were fed or sheltered. A numbers game quickly develops to justify the continuation of the services. The more people are served, the more the service is needed. The programs become institutionalized and that demand the clients need what is being offered rather than offering what the clients need. This has become the way in which agencies grow and survive. Rather than maintaining the flexibility necessary to meet individual needs, programs seek to justify their existence by registering as many people as possible. When this happens, programs and organizations cease to function for the homeless and exist only to perpetuate themselves. While the original intentions were good, the end result reduces the homeless to little more than numbers. In fact, many homeless individuals refuse to reside in shelters for this very reason. They claim to have too much dignity to be treated like cattle in a roundup.

A person who works with the homeless once interviewed a homeless mother with two children. The homeless woman meekly sat answering the barrage of questions that come with any request for services. The social worker helped the woman fill out the appropriate forms for Aid to Families with Dependent Children, food stamps, and public housing assistance. After the lengthy applications were completed (and prior to sending the family to three different social service agencies to deliver the applications), she asked if there was anything else she could do to help. The homeless mother thanked the woman for all her efforts, saying how great it would be if she received benefits, but what she really needed were Pampers. She didn't have any more, and she was most concerned about a diaper long overdue for changing. The agency, of course, had no diapers. Unfortunately, this scenario is typical.

An appropriate response to the homeless should begin with the most pressing needs, as identified by the homeless themselves. We must learn to listen. Just as a doctor first listens to the symptoms described by the patient, those who seek to help the homeless must first listen to discover the most pressing needs—which are rarely what we first think. Listening to the homeless is very difficult. Many are, as O'Rourke claims, substance abusers, and they will seek ways to gain drugs or alcohol. Until these individuals reach the point where they really want to change, there is little that can be done for them. Nevertheless, they should be identified and confronted with their substance abuse whenever possible. This will cause many to shy away from such confrontations at the shelters, thereby freeing up staff to concentrate on those who want to help themselves. When homeless substance abusers are ready to confront their problems, detoxification and in-patient treatment programs should be immediately made available. Once these interventions are completed, referral should be made to smaller residential treatment programs. These eight-to-twelve-bed facilities house only people who have completed in-patient programs, which allows for the development of a social support system with individuals sharing a common problem. Each is required to attend daily meetings of Alcoholics Anonymous, treatment programs, or individual counseling sessions. In addition, each person is required to secure employment within thirty days. If these conditions are not met, the resident must leave. Individuals in recovery may remain in the program for up to two years and may leave when they feel capable of maintaining an alcohol- or drug-free life.

This approach to helping homeless substance abusers help themselves is a key to responding to anyone who requests services from a shelter. Regardless of the reasons a person is homeless, that person must first feel as though he or she is being heard. The person can then be confronted with the reality of his or her situation. Those seeking to help the homeless must hear and then mirror the situation back, as most are in denial that they are homeless. People simply do not want to admit they are homeless. A sense of dignity leads homeless individuals to separate themselves from the hundreds of homeless people who will sleep in the same room that night. The homeless thus must first be heard before they can begin to accept the reality of their situation. In his novel *Brightness Falls*, Jay McInerney describes the illusion a homeless man lives on the streets:

> *Ace felt hot, the mojo was on him tonight for certain. Feinting at shadows with his new gloves, he paused on the Bowery, trying to feel his luck. Like*

many on the street, Ace was a fatalist. Whatever was going to be would be. You just had to try not to get in the way of it. Coming up on a dude in a suit, he asked for a quarter. The man passed him by like the Invisible Man, but Ace was used to that, people not hearing and not seeing him, the normal citizenry equipped with that streamlined New York tunnel vision—eyes straight ahead and focused on the next stop lest the gaze get snagged on something ugly—equipped with radar that registered his presence as an obstacle to be avoided like a rock or a pile of dog shit. It could be such a bitch that sometimes you almost yearned for the straight thing, and yet he found a certain romance in this business of pure subsistence, foraging and hunting like the early pioneers in a hostile landscape, that was far more exciting than flipping burgers, hunting furniture, riding his ass all over the city on a bike delivering messages.[3]

For most, being homeless means never being heard. Even those who seek to help them, social workers and ministers who help comprise the "normal citizenry," often listen only for that information which will satisfy the needs of their program, ministry, or institution. The first step toward helping the homeless is hearing them and reflecting the consistencies and inconsistencies of who they are back at them. This is the only way in which the homeless may begin to understand who they truly are. It is also the first step in establishing accountability.

Just as substance abusers must admit that they have hit bottom and have no control over their addiction, so must the homeless recognize that they are at the very bottom of society. They can descend no lower. The reasons for their condition do not matter at this point—those reasons may be overcome only after they are ready to face their problem. They must first see themselves as homeless. Those seeking to help the homeless must help them to see that such a life style is not acceptable. The numerous systemic conditions that make for homelessness must be addressed, of course, but once someone is already on the streets, it is entirely a personal matter.

The war against homelessness, as stated earlier, is a both/and and not an either/or situation. Since the early 1980s, many have argued that people are homeless either because they chose such a life or because systemic conditions made them so. "The conservatives among us refused to believe that the homeless were homeless because they didn't have homes," O'Rourke writes. "And liberals refused to believe that rent control, bad mores and civil rights for [the mentally ill] were what turned the homeless out-of-doors."[4] Both sides are right, of course, but neither is willing to admit it. As a result, people continue to find themselves in shelters for lack of other housing options, and the policies that create homelessness continue to be advocated.

Once an individual admits that he or she is homeless and then decides not to choose such a life, the possibility of genuine assistance is possible. The homeless must not only come to an understanding of their homelessness, they must also comprehend that they have the power to do something about it. They do not have to become fatalistic. There is no more important task for those seeking to help the homeless than to facilitate this understanding. It is a more difficult task than it may seem. People who are fatalistic have little sense of hope. Without hope, it is hard to believe things will get better. Those with hope are easy to spot in the shelter or on the streets. They take advantage of every opportunity made available to them. They are willing to do whatever is asked of them. They say thank you. They smile. They are also in the minority. Without a sense of hope, however, the homeless will always be homeless. The atmosphere of the shelter and the attitude of those seeking to help must foster hope.

Hope cannot be engendered without the creation of a sense of self-worth and dignity. "Our sense of self-worth and dignity is rooted in our being needed, if not by our parents then by someone else who values who we are," writes Dorothy Soelle.[5] Shelters must become places that not only serve the homeless but also establish a sense of partnership with them. The homeless must become co-workers in the operation of the shelter—they can then enhance their sense of hope and self-worth, gain from this practical experience, and be held accountable for overcoming life on the streets. These goals are accomplished by grounding the shelter in community, not charity.

Shelter staff should balance holding the homeless accountable with making them feel included in the operation of the program. The homeless can begin by caring for the building itself. To remain in the shelter, the homeless should be required to clean, wash linens, unload deliveries, perform yard work. Shelters must not merely be places to eat, sleep, and, hopefully, wash. After mastering these basic tasks, the homeless should begin cooking, answering phones, helping run the office, and offering general support to the professional staff. Not only do these tasks allow the homeless to feel included, but they also teach them skills necessary for any job. No shelter should employ someone to answer the phones when the homeless are available to do it.

Shelter staff must concentrate their energies on supervising the homeless, offering constructive criticism and overall support for the individuals doing the work. This also means that the professional staff must be willing to get their own hands dirty, lest they be viewed more as wardens than partners. The important point here is that the shelter must become the vehicle through which the homeless are transported back into the mainstream of society. Any other goal, no matter how worthy, does little more than enable a homeless life style to continue.

Meeting the basic food, shelter, and hygienic needs of the homeless accomplishes little more than allowing them to continue to exist. Shelters must develop creative programs that enable the homeless to immediately take action against their plight. The development of nonprofit labor pools is a tactic that can help the homeless accomplish many of their goals. Using the men residing in the shelter as the target population, the labor pool begins with those self-motivated individuals who exhibit the determination to help. A "hire the homeless" program is announced, and shelter staff call on area businesses that may be in need of temporary labor. The resulting referrals mean immediate work for the homeless. Shelters should act as more than mere referral sources, however, and actually enter into work contracts with the businesses. They should charge the businesses a small administrative fee for placing the homeless on the job. In meeting their own labor needs, the companies also know that they are giving the homeless an opportunity to work. The homeless individuals get paid and, coupled with a life-skills program, are able to learn how to manage and save their money. Shelters may even make enough to diminish their reliance on government grants. Those who work with the homeless must cultivate new and better ways to enable those who can to reenter the mainstream of society. Even if shelters fail in these endeavors, they will easily be able to resume their traditional activities with little risk of alienating their base of support.

For shelters to be specific about their goals, the shotgun approach of assisting as many homeless people as possible must be abandoned. Just as hospitals often emphasize certain specialties, shelters must focus on particular segments of the homeless population. Shelters seeking to serve the unemployed or underemployed must have an in-depth understanding of the job market in their community and prepare the homeless for those particular jobs. Offering the basic services of food and housing during the evenings, shelters can direct their energies during the day toward enhancing residents' employability and job-search skills. The homeless unemployed often have additional barriers to employment, such as not having an address, a lack of access to a telephone, difficulties in maintaining good hygiene, shortages of appropriate attire, and no transportation to interviews. Shelters should direct their interventions toward overcoming these obstacles. Finding the job is often the easiest part, however, and the professional staff must be willing to continue offering support after employment. According to the National Alliance to End Homelessness, "Even if a homeless person manages to get a job, he or she must make a mighty effort to adjust to working conditions, because the culture of the workplace may have become alien to the isolated, brutal world that homeless people live in."[6] Postemployment counseling must be available until the transition to the job is complete. Once the individual is comfortable in his or her job duties, the passage to independent housing may begin.

Shelters targeting the mentally ill should also begin with the basic services of food, housing, and clothing. Intensive supervision must be provided for residents with acute needs. "The ultimate goal," write John Talbott and Richard Lamb, "must be to insure that each chronically mentally ill person . . . has one person—such as a case manager or a resource manager—who is responsible for his or her treatment."[7] General medical assessment and care must be available in the shelter. Crisis services must be accessible, so the shelters must have a working relationship with hospitals and other organizations that work exclusively with the mentally ill. While shelters are capable of housing those homeless mentally ill who are in a stable condition, those in crisis must be referred to agencies providing more intensive treatment and care.

The American Psychiatric Association suggests that there are three tiers of shelter services needed for the homeless mentally ill. First, basic emergency shelters are necessary to get them off the streets. Second, transitional accommodations, a step up from emergency shelters, are required to assess and address the various needs of the population. Such a setting allows the mentally ill to prepare for independent living. Third, long-term supportive residences are needed "where privacy and independence are afforded residents and where assistance in obtaining services in times of need is assured."[8]

Shelters can also gear their programs toward work with

homeless groups such as substance abusers, women, families with children, those struggling to live with AIDS, and the illiterate. By using the basic services of food, housing, and clothing as the starting point, shelters can concentrate on the needs of any specific homeless population. Such action ensures a better use of shelter resources, getting closer to the exact needs of specific populations. Genuine assistance is much more likely to occur when shelters target certain groups of homeless individuals.

The nature of the work with homeless individuals forces shelter employees to juggle the separate goals of accountability, flexibility, and the development of a social support system. They must hold the homeless accountable to the fact that homelessness is an unacceptable life style. Those working with the homeless also must be flexible to make interventions personal enough to meet the needs of the different individuals. These interventions must be performed in the context of helping the homeless learn, or relearn, how to function as part of a social support system. Homeless individuals may even form support groups in an effort to hold one another accountable and to develop a safety-in-numbers feeling.

Such an approach will mean an overhaul of the current shelter system, downsizing shelters and establishing a much more personable atmosphere. As pointed out before, the goal is quality, not quantity. Shelters should not exist for those who choose to be homeless. New shelters should be designed for those who do not choose such a life, providing the appropriate mechanism by which to leave the streets.

The current system of support does not allow for the development of a new way of sheltering. The vast majority of public and private support fosters shelters that enable homelessness. To get serious about reducing the homeless population, the church, government, and private efforts must piece together the fragmented delivery of assistance to those working with the homeless. The Interagency Council on Homelessness must not only discuss how it

allocates funds but make certain that its awards complement one another, forging a comprehensive battle plan. The
allocation process, filtering down to the local level through
numerous units of federal, state, and local government,
each with its own agenda, must develop and work for a
common goal. Rather than each unit of government establishing its own homeless programs, public funds should be
given to the local shelters. These shelters could then have,
on-site, the personnel and programs necessary to immediately assist the homeless. Medical clinics, classroom training, case management, job training, job search and placement services, parenting skills classes, nutrition classes, and
other necessary forms of intervention would all be immediately accessible. Shelters could treat the social ill of homelessness much like hospitals treat physical ills.

It appears that government funding sources have finally
learned that the war on homelessness cannot be won unless
the troops are united. Kevin Phillips predicts in his book
The Politics of Rich and Poor that "the 1990s [will] be a time
. . . to correct the excesses of the 1980s, for the dangers
posed by excessive individualism, greed and insufficient
concern for America as a community went beyond the issue of fairness."[9] There now seems to be a genuine effort by
government to use public monies to foster cooperative and
coordinated efforts at the local level. It is interesting to note,
however, that the government is calling on local groups to
do what it is not willing to do itself. The various
government-funded social services still do not work together, although they are more than willing to tell local agencies
to coordinate their efforts. Until the different branches of
government learn to cooperate with each other, however,
much of the energy spent to solve the homeless problem
will be wasted.

The strict separation of church- and state-sponsored efforts must also end. Currently, the majority of shelters in
the United States were founded or are sponsored by religious institutions. Government funding is thus restricted,
lest it be used to propagate religious values and beliefs.

While there is certainly cause to closely monitor how religious groups spend government funds, there is no reason to believe that churches and synagogues cannot fulfill their mandates to care for the poor through the shelter system while leaving the conversion of souls to the voluntary worship services already in place. Churches, by and large, already benefit from the government through their nonprofit status, various public services, special tax breaks, and, on occasion, outright financial assistance. The current system often makes for a duplication of effort, something the government claims to despise yet fosters through its allocation of money.

Obviously the religious community must take responsibility for caring for the poor, but how? The religious leadership, by and large, has its own agenda—perpetuating the institution. Should the response then come from lay people? How does one awaken this tremendous resource? How can the mandates of Scripture empower congregations to meet the needs of the homeless they encounter? The religious community has responded to the homeless by offering some basic services and by claiming its concern for them in prayers, sermons, hymns, but it has yet to attain the level of commitment necessary to make a significant difference. "For it takes commitment to take care of them until they are better," Noah Snider writes. "Like the example of the Samaritan, we must bind their wounds, provide their place of rest and safety, and support them until they are healed. And each one will require a varied amount of time and expense both financially and psychologically."[10]

The religious community has been long on verbiage but short on action. Proclamation without demonstration is little more than cheap talk. Churches and synagogues must "stay with them, teach them to be productive, make use of them but not use them. We must be patient, understanding that many of the homeless are crippled, skeptical of our promises and our purpose. We must be prepared to never hear a thank you except from the one who *commanded* that we take care of them."[11] The religious community is free to pursue God's vision of a just and humane world. The only requirement is a personal investment on the part of the congregation. Until the religious community quits talking and begins to act in ways other than superficial "ministries" to meet basic needs, the homeless will continue to view them skeptically, and God will likely view them with disdain.

Local efforts to deal with homelessness must be coordinated in a common effort involving all segments of the community. Groups already working must include other segments of the community that have expressed concern, either negative or positive, about homelessness. The active participation and inclusion of all appropriate organizations, units of government, agencies, and citizens is needed if this complex social problem is going to be successfully addressed. Getting such groups to work in concert is often a most arduous task. Someone must take charge, however, and invest whatever is needed to get county and city municipalities, numerous social service agencies, religious groups, business organizations, and individual citizens together in order to respond to homelessness. It will take the creativity, energy, and resources of each group to forge a suitable response. Often, it will not be possible to get everyone involved. Many will be unable to overcome their negative stereotypes of the homeless. This should not discourage those who are working to develop a comprehensive strategy, however, as any networking will likely improve the situation.

Too often, when diverse groups gather to discuss problems, they divide into two sides: theirs and ours. Because of this, advocates make the mistake of getting into fights they have no chance of winning and thus risk alienating the very people who can help them most. To prevent this from happening, Gregory F. Pierce suggests the use of a power analysis, which is little more than a large sheet of paper listing the "names of all the major institutions or individuals who do—or possibly could—influence the decisions being made in the community." All of the major community organizations, units of government, and people with power would be listed. Circles would be drawn "around each name, indicating by their size the relative strength of each of the names on the paper." While this may be a subjective exercise, it identifies those players who are most important. "Lines between each of the names, [indicate] where relationships occur and what the nature of the relationship— both positive and negative—might be."[12] This exercise develops a clear sense of the people and organizations most needed to effectively impact homelessness at the local level, providing a focused guide to action.

After the principal players have been identified and they begin meeting, meaningful dialogue can begin. There will be much give and take in these discussions as boundary lines are established by the various organizations and individuals. It is important to recognize the limitations of those involved. Governmental regulations, agency purpose, and personal preference may prevent some from taking on tasks that they seem perfectly suited for. To address all aspects of the problem, individuals and groups must be forged into a working coalition. The typical approach is to sell everyone a need. For example, to get results, according to Peter Drucker, "say, 'These are the results. This is what we can do for you.'"[13] The complexities of homelessness can be addressed only if the appropriate people are working together to respond to the problems. This includes viewing homelessness from all perspectives held in the community. For example, while advocates may be concerned with providing additional shelter space to people living on the streets, residents may by anxious about the negative impact of homelessness in their neighborhood. The goal is to find common ground and then involve the entire community in forging a common, working response.

While numerous programs are already available to the homeless, the current system of delivering these services often becomes a barrier to needed assistance. To overcome these problems, some, but not all, of those who work with the homeless meet regularly to discuss the needs of individual clients. Often, the purpose of these meetings is not to coordinate activities but to discuss an individual's multiple problems and whether one helper is more suited than another to offer direction through a short-term crisis.

Perhaps these informal coalitions could evolve into homeless authorities. Authorities would be better equipped to accomplish several tasks: (1) develop a comprehensive plan for public and private agencies to effectively deal with the problems of the homeless in a particular community; (2) coordinate, evaluate, and provide the administrative services and assistance needed to implement the plan; and (3) contract with the public and private agencies to provide the programs and services developed by the plan.

By formalizing institutional relationships, the homeless authorities could ensure that the appropriate agencies and organizations were working in concert. Representatives of city and county governments, the Department of Labor, the local board of education, the state Department of Human Resources, the state Housing Department, the local housing authority, the local shelter and service providers, and concerned citizens would constitute an appropriate alliance to address the delivery of services.

Working as an umbrella agency responsible for the coordination of homeless services in the community, a local homeless authority could establish working relationships with each of the various organizations involved in homeless issues. When problems surface concerning a matter relating to homelessness, they could be brought to the attention of the authority by service providers, homeless advocates, local governments, concerned citizens, and the homeless themselves. To resolve the problem or attend to the issue at hand, the authority could engage the resources of the necessary parties and encourage joint decision making. This inclusive approach would enable the authority to address concerns voiced by many different organizations in a collective manner. As a result, the social services community would be viewed by the public as a cohesive group, with individual agencies combining knowledge, skills, and resources for a common purpose. Shelters and service providers, under the auspices of the authority, could work together and pursue joint ventures when gaps in services were identified.

Perhaps most controversially, the authority could be given the task of allocating all government funds—local, state, and federal—earmarked for homeless programs. This would enable the community to know that a reputable watchdog is preventing the duplication of services and ensuring that the money is spent to assist the homeless. Many agencies would not want to give such power to the authority, being more concerned with their own survival than with what actually works. This is all the more reason that all funds should flow through a central representative body.

Homelessness is a complex social problem, encompassing numerous social ills and multiple subpopulations with specific and individual needs. The response so far has been well-intentioned but has often enabled the problem rather than attacked it. Various groups reacting to homelessness, working independently, have not effectively helped the situation. Until these attempts are fashioned into a common effort, bringing together the strengths of the government, the religious community, the service agencies, and the homeless themselves, the problem will continue. Why don't the homeless have homes? Because the organizations and individuals working to help the homeless haven't learned how to address the total problem.

Jim Beaty of the Atlanta Task Force for the Homeless imagines what would happen if a massive fire broke out in any community in the country. The fire would decimate housing, forcing families into the streets. They would lose all of their worldly possessions, perhaps even their livelihoods. What would be the response? There would be an enormous outpouring of compassion by the rest of the community. Public services would put out the fire, organize temporary shelter, make provisions for food, analyze why the fire started, and institute policies to reduce the risk of it ever occurring again. Citizens would collect clothing, donate money, and open their own homes to care for those who were burned out. Private companies would make resources available to accomplish these things. The entire community would come together to meet the needs of their own. Why then can't homelessness be approached the same way?

Help is often given only to those who are perceived to be worthy of people's time, money, and compassion. Many people simply do not believe that the homeless deserve their efforts. The homeless thus receive some attention, enough to get by, but few of them are able to gather the resources necessary to resume their pursuit of the American Dream. Until enough people believe that homelessness should not exist, the homeless will not have homes.

NOTES

INTRODUCTION

1. Alice S. Baum and Donald W. Burns, *A Nation in Denial: The Truth about Homelessness* (forthcoming), as cited by William Raspberry in "Truth about Homelessness?" *Columbus Ledger-Journal*, December 26, 1992.

2. For more on this congregation, see Micheal Elliott, *The Society of Salty Saints* (New York: Crossroad, 1987).

3. Micheal Elliott, *The Community of the Abandoned* (New York: Crossroad, 1989), xi.

4. Ibid.

5. Micheal Elliott, *Partners in Grace* (Cleveland: The Pilgrim Press, 1992), 15–16.

6. Rush Limbaugh, *The Way Things Ought To Be* (New York: Pocket Books, 1992), 250.

CHAPTER 1

1. Noah Snider, *When There's No Place Like Home* (Nashville: Thomas Nelson Publishers, 1991).

2. Anna Faith Jones, ed., *Homelessness: Critical Issues for Policy and Practice* (Boston: The Boston Foundation, 1987), 4.

3. National Alliance to End Homelessness, *What You Can Do To Help the Homeless* (New York: A Fireside Book, 1991), 12.

4. Alan Keith-Lucas, *Giving and Taking Help* (Chapel Hill: The University of North Carolina Press, 1972).

CHAPTER 2

1. Mary Ellen Hombs and Mitch Snyder, *Homelessness in America* (Washington, D.C.: The Community for Creative Nonviolence, 1983), xvi.

2. Jay Mathews, "Rethinking Homeless Myths," *Newsweek*, April 6, 1992, 29.

3. Nels Anderson, *The Hobo* (Chicago: The University of Chicago Press, 1923), 89.

4. Deirdre Carmody, "City to Spend $100 Million on Homeless," *New York Times*, October 10, 1984.

5. Jonathan Kozol, *Rachel and Her Children* (New York: Crown Publishers, 1988), 4.

6. Georgia Department of Human Resources and the Chatham-Savannah Youth Futures Authority, "Family-focused Early Intervention Project" (unpublished concept paper, 1991).

7. Alice Brussiere et al., "Homeless Women and Children," *Clearinghouse Review* (Special Issue, 1991): 433.

8. Ellen L. Bassuk, Alison S. Laruiat, and Lenore Rubin, "Homeless Families," in *Homelessness: Critical Issues*, 23.

9. Georgia Department of Human Resources and the Chatham-Savannah Youth Futures Authority, "Family-focused Early Intervention Project."

10. Stephen L. Wobido et al., "Outreach," in *Under the Safety Net*, ed. Philip W. Brickner (New York: Norton Books, 1990), 330.

CHAPTER 3

1. Catherine Zudak, "Fragmented Approach to Homelessness," *Public Management* (March 1992): 9.

2. David Ellis, "Star of His Own Sad Comedy," *Time*, March 9, 1992, 63.

3. Frederick Buechner, *Wishful Thinking* (San Francisco: Harper and Row, 1973), 73.

4. Peter Senge, *The Fifth Discipline* (New York: Doubleday, 1990), 111.

5. Peter Drucker, *Managing the Nonprofit Organization* (New York: HarperCollins, 1990), 152.

6. Joseph Alsop, *FDR: A Centenary Remembrance* (New York: The Viking Press, 1982), 143.

7. John N. Lozier, Mandy Johnson, and Joan Haynes, "Overcoming Troubled Relationships between Programs and the Community," in *Under the Safety Net*, 32.

CHAPTER 4

1. Gayle White, "Jimmy Carter's Challenge to Religion," *Atlanta Constitution*, April 19, 1992.

2. Snider, *No Place*, 136.

3. John H. Elliott, *A Home for the Homeless* (Philadelphia: Fortress Press, 1981), 49.

4. Wayne Meeks, *The First Urban Christians* (New Haven: Yale University Press, 1983).

5. White, "Jimmy Carter's Challenge."

6. Francis M. Dubose, *How Churches Grow in an Urban World* (Nashville: Broadman Press, 1978), 58–78.

7. White, "Jimmy Carter's Challenge."

8. Louis Smith and Joseph Barndt, *Beyond Brokenness* (New York: Friendship Press, 1980), 108.

9. David Claerbaut, *Urban Ministry* (Grand Rapids: Zondervan, 1983), 94.

10. Hombs and Snyder, *Homelessness in America*, 76.

11. Dieter T. Hessel, *Social Ministry* (Philadelphia: The Westminster Press, 1982), 16.

12. E. Glenn Hinson, *The Integrity of the Church* (Nashville: Broadman Press, 1978), 150.

13. Kenneth Leech, *The Social God* (London: Sheldon Press, 1981), 102.

14. Hinson, *The Integrity*, 151.

15. Larry T. McSwain, "The Cultural Captivity of Urban Churches," in *The Urban Challenge*, ed. Larry L. Rose and C. Kirk Hadaway (Nashville: Broadman Press, 1982), 58–59.

16. Ibid., 60.

17. Dolores Leckey, "Sacred Shelters: Families and Spiritual Empowerment," in *Living with Apocalypse*, ed. Tilden Edwards (San Francisco: Harper & Row, 1984), 180.

18. Michael Roschke, "The Gifted Urban Lay Person," in *Metro Ministry*, ed. David Frenchak and Sharrel Keyes (Elgin, Ill.: David C. Cook Publishing, 1979), 160.

19. Ibid.

CHAPTER 5

1. Amy Haus, ed., *Working with Homeless People* (New York: New York Department of Social Services, 1988), 101.

2. Zudak, "Fragmented Approach," 9.

3. Millard Fuller and Linda Fuller, *The Excitement Is Building* (Dallas: Word Publishing, 1990), 116.

4. Frederick Buechner, *Now and Then* (San Francisco: Harper & Row, 1983), 29.

5. Snider, *No Place*, 238–39.

6. Gregory F. Pierce, *Activism That Makes Sense* (New York: Paulist Press, 1984), 59.

7. Warren Bennis and Burt Nanus, *Leaders* (New York: Harper & Row, 1985), 43.

8. Drucker, *Managing*, 21.

CHAPTER 6

1. P. J. O'Rourke, *Parliament of Whores* (New York: First Vintage Books, 1992), 190.

2. Ibid., 191.

3. Jay McInerney, *Brightness Falls* (New York: Alfred A. Knopf, 1992), 86–87.

4. O'Rourke, *Parliament of Whores*, 33.

5. Dorothy Soelle with Shirley A. Cloyes, *To Work and To Love* (Philadelphia: Fortress Press, 1994), 16.

6. National Alliance to End Homelessness, *What You Can Do*, 57.

7. John A. Talbott and H. Richard Lamb, "Summary and Recommendations," in *The Homeless Mentally Ill*, ed. H. Richard Lamb (Washington, D.C.: American Psychiatric Association, 1984), 7.

8. Ibid., 129.

9. Kevin Phillips, *The Politics of Rich and Poor* (New York: Random House, 1990), 200–201.

10. Snider, *No Place*, 141.

11. Ibid., 141–42.

12. Pierce, *Activism*, 39.

13. Drucker, *Managing*, 100.

SELECTED
BIBLIOGRAPHY

Alsop, Joseph. *FDR: A Centenary Remembrance*. New York: The Viking Press, 1982.

Anderson, Nels. *The Hobo*. Chicago: The University of Chicago Press, 1923.

Bennis, Warren, and Burt Nanus. *Leaders*. New York: Harper & Row, 1985.

Brickner, Philip W., ed. *Under the Safety Net*. New York: Norton Books, 1990.

Buechner, Frederick. *Now and Then*. San Francisco: Harper & Row, 1983.

———. *Wishful Thinking*. San Francisco: Harper & Row, 1973.

Claerbaut, David. *Urban Ministry*. Grand Rapids: Zondervan, 1983.

Drucker, Peter. *Managing the Nonprofit Organization*. New York: HarperCollins, 1990.

Dubose, Francis M. *How Churches Grow in an Urban World*. Nashville: Broadman Press, 1978.

Elliott, John H. *A Home for the Homeless*. Philadelphia: Fortress Press, 1981.

Elliott, Micheal. *The Community of the Abandoned*. New York: Crossroad, 1989.

———. *Partners in Grace*. Cleveland: The Pilgrim Press, 1992.

———. *The Society of Salty Saints*. New York: Crossroad, 1987.

Fuller, Millard, and Linda Fuller. *The Excitement Is Building*. Dallas: Word Publishing, 1990.

Haus, Amy, ed. *Working with Homeless People*. New York: New York Department of Social Services, 1988.

Hessel, Dieter T. *Social Ministry*. Philadelphia: The Westminster Press, 1982.

Hinson, E. Glenn. *The Integrity of the Church*. Nashville: Broadman Press, 1978.

Hombs, Mary Ellen, and Mitch Snyder. *Homelessness in America*. Washington, D.C.: The Community for Creative Nonviolence, 1983.

Jones, Anna Faith, ed. *Homelessness: Critical Issues for Policy and Practice*. Boston: The Boston Foundation, 1987.

Keith-Lucas, Alan. *Giving and Taking Help*. Chapel Hill: The University of North Carolina Press, 1972.

Kozol, Jonathan. *Rachel and Her Children*. New York: Crown Publishers, 1988.

Lamb, H. Richard, ed. *The Homeless Mentally Ill*. Washington, D.C.: American Psychiatric Association, 1984.

Leckey, Dolores. *Living with Apocalypse*. Tilden Edwards, ed. San Francisco: Harper & Row, 1984.

Leech, Kenneth. *The Social God*. London: Sheldon Press, 1981.

Limbaugh, Rush. *The Way Things Ought To Be*. New York: Pocket Books, 1992.

McInerney, Jay. *Brightness Falls*. New York: Alfred A. Knopf, 1992.

McSwain, Larry T. "The Cultural Captivity of Urban Churches." In *The Urban Challenge*. Larry L. Rose and C. Kirk Hadaway, eds. Nashville: Broadman Press, 1982.

Meeks, Wayne. *The First Urban Christians*. New Haven: Yale University Press, 1983.

National Alliance to End Homelessness. *What You Can Do To Help the Homeless*. New York: A Fireside Book, 1991.

O'Rourke, P. J. *Parliament of Whores*. New York: First Vintage Books, 1992.

Phillips, Kevin. *The Politics of Rich and Poor*. New York: Random House, 1990.

Pierce, Gregory F. *Activism That Makes Sense*. New York: Paulist Press, 1984.

Roschke, Michael. "The Gifted Urban Lay Person." In *Metro Ministry*. David Frenchak and Sharrel Keyes, eds. Elgin, Ill.: David C. Cook Publishing, 1979.

Senge, Peter. *The Fifth Discipline*. New York: Doubleday, 1990.

Smith, Louis, and Joseph Barndt. *Beyond Brokenness*. New York: Friendship Press, 1980.

Snider, Noah. *When There's No Place Like Home*. Nashville: Thomas Nelson Publishers, 1991.

Soelle, Dorothy, with Shirley A. Cloyes. *To Work and To Love*. Philadelphia: Fortress Press, 1994.

INDEX

DATE DUE

NOV 2 9 1998	FEB 0 5 2011		
APR 3 0 2001			
MAY 0 8 REC'D NOV 2 2 2009			
OCT 3 1 2001			
FEB 2 4 2002			
MAR 0 1 REC'D			
APR 2 2 2002			
APR 1 1 REC'D			
NOV 0 2 2002			
NOV 0 8 REC'D			
OCT 2 5 2004			
OCT 1 1 REC'D			
NOV 0 5 2008			
DEC 0 9 REC'D			
NOV 0 4 2009			
NOV 3 0 REC'D			
GAYLORD			PRINTED IN U.S.A.